"Speaking as someone who's passionate about helping people make better decisions and live with fewer regrets, this book by Chris Conlee is a game-changer. Simplify your life right now by reading it and applying the radically simple truths to every relationship you have. You'll quickly discover that love works!"

Andy Stanley, author, communicator, and founder of North Point Ministries

"*Love Works* is an outstanding combination of inspiration and instruction. Every chapter stirs emotions, challenges intellect, and inspires action. Perhaps most importantly, though, is that every reader receives the confidence and commitment to prove through their own life that, indeed, love works."

John O'Leary, #1 national bestselling author of *On Fire*

"LOVE. It's more than a feeling. It's practical and it works. Yes, there is work that love does. And when love is *not* working, it shuts down the relationship factory. Relational unemployment rises, leading to relational bankruptcy. There is good news! My friend Chris Conlee's book *Love Works* reopens the shutdown relationship factory and offers love full employment. Love works!"

Sam Chand, leadership consultant and author of *Bigger Faster Leadership*

"*Love Works* is the powerful story of a church impacting the city of Memphis and a pastor living out the power of love in a practical and action-oriented way. Chris Conlee doesn't just talk about love—he lives it. It's time for all of us to put love into action, and there's no better guide than Chris."

Brad Lomenick, former president of Catalyst and author of *H3 Leadership* and *The Catalyst Leader*

"Everyone talks about love, but Chris shows us the way to make love work. Read this book and let God's love transform the way you live and love."

Jon Gordon, bestselling author of *The Carpenter* and *Training Camp*

"*Love Works* is the real deal. For those of us who have experienced heartbreak, Chris takes a good, hard look at how the love of Jesus works. Like, really works. If you know nothing about Jesus or everything about him, you'll find this to be true: the story is gripping, the love is real. Give this book the time it's due and it might just transform your life."

Carey Nieuwhof, founding pastor of Connexus Church

"This is perhaps the greatest book on God's love that has ever been written. Please read it today and I promise you won't be able to put it down . . . and you'll never be the same again. Chris, God has given you incredible insight. What a gift you've given us in this book! Thanks for your faithfulness."

Jim Blanchard, chairman, board of advisors, JBA Capital, LLC

"I always want to know what kind of person is behind the message of a particular book. While I cannot know that about most authors, I do indeed know what kind of man Chris Conlee is. He's a man of character, passion, integrity, and focus. He's a truly great leader and pastor. And he has written an excellent book here . . . not just because it's readable, practical, biblical, and doable, but because Chris himself embodies the ethic of *Love Works*."

Dr. Clayton King, teaching pastor at Newspring Church, executive editor of *Youth Worker Magazine*, and author of *Overcome* and *Stronger*

"Chris and his church have taught me and my team about how love works with their partnership with Overton High School in Memphis. I've shared his story over and over again: how a church fell in love with the students and teachers at an unlikely school and showed up in real, tangible ways to demonstrate that love works. This is just one example of many Chris shares in this book of what it really means to be there for your neighbor when it matters the most."

Reggie Joiner, founder and CEO of Orange

"If you enjoyed *The Cure*, we highly recommend *Love Works*. It is refreshing in its honesty in articulating a recurring problem in our world: when we're not loved well, nothing works well. This book paints a picture of God's love that is irresistible. You will walk away from this book believing wholeheartedly that only love works."

Dr. Bruce McNicol, John Lynch, and Bill Thrall, coauthors of *The Cure*, *The Cure & Parents*, and *The Ascent of a Leader*, and partners at Trueface

"As a player and coach in the NBA for approximately forty years, I can recognize a great coach when I see one. Chris Conlee is an inspirational life coach, especially when it comes to teaching us about God's love. This book is a must-read. Love works!"

Lionel Hollins, former NBA player and coach; founder and CEO of I Train Fundamentals, LLC, and Lionel Hollins Charities

"As someone who's worked closely with Chris as a leader and friend for nearly two decades, I can say beyond a shadow of a doubt that Chris authentically lives the message of this book better than

anyone I know. *Love Works* is the life-blood pumping through the heart of Highpoint Church. Likewise, this book will give you, your relationships, and your faith new life and hope."

Andy Savage, cofounder and teaching pastor of Highpoint Church, Memphis, TN

"If love hasn't worked perfectly for you, read this book. Chris Conlee is both a thought-provoking teacher and a master storyteller. He'll wisely jostle your priorities and gently jar your emotions until you see how love can work. Sit with Chris through these pages and you'll find your heart recharged and your life renewed."

Craig Springer, executive director of Alpha USA

"In his new book, Chris nails it with this big idea: love works. At the John Maxwell Foundation, we teach our members how to love well: love their employees, love their customers, love their staff, and—get this—even love their competitors. We have found that love works, especially with those who don't love you. Love well."

Terence Chatmon, president of the John Maxwell Foundation and Equip Leadership

"Pastor Chris teaches a mathematical equation that most of us never learned in school: Love God + Love People = Love Works. The number-one common denominator in our lives is to live for others instead of living for ourselves. If you can do this math, it will change your life and the lives of the people around you."

Tommy Spaulding, two-time *New York Times* bestselling author of *The Heart-Led Leader* and *It's Not Just Who You Know*

"*Love Works* is the epitome of a DIY manual for loving boldly. Putting these concepts to work will change your life and your circle of influence. This is one of the best books I've ever read!"

Amy Howard, CEO of Amy Howard at Home and author of *A Maker's Guide*

"*Love Works* will change your perspective on the power, persistence, and performance of love. It will take you on a journey from where you are to where you can go to experience how love works in your own life. Chris Conlee not only wrote this book but he has lived it! *Love Works* will be a life-changing book for every reader."

Phyllis Hennecy Hendry, president and CEO of Lead Like Jesus

"*Love Works* will show you how to unleash the power of love in every relationship. Love produces genuine success. I know and love this author. He lives what he writes. Digest and apply this content and watch love change your life and the lives of all those in your sphere of influence."

Steve Gaines, PhD, senior pastor of Bellevue Baptist Church, Memphis, TN, and president of the Southern Baptist Convention

"Chris Conlee is a man who believes and lives out 'the greatest of these is love.' In *Love Works* he provides compelling evidence of how we as the church, by prioritizing love, can emphatically serve as the hands and feet of Jesus. I see Chris apply Christ's command to 'love God and love people' in multiple arenas . . . from the church and the community to working with executives to build the next generation of values-based leaders. This book is a game-changer!"

David Alexander, president and CEO of TruGreen

"Chris Conlee has a message for people: love works. He's not just writing a book suggesting the next magic puzzle piece that will fix our Christian life. Instead, he writes to hurting people, discouraged people, hopeless people . . . reminding them that, no matter how often they've seen love fail, love works. And no logical argument is going to convince a hopeless person, so Chris uses the most persuasive tool available to us: story. He shares story after story of how the One who is Love works. It was wonderful for me to hear stories from Memphis, from Highpoint Church, and from those for whom Love has worked."

Todd Agnew, worship leader, singer, and songwriter

"*Love Works* brings a new vibrancy and practical wisdom to a subject we have all too often domesticated and made tame. Using stories and an approach to the Bible that brings out many refreshing insights, Chris offers a powerful tool for the transfiguration of lives, leading to the transformation of society."

Rev. Dr. Russ Parker, author of *Healing Wounded History* and founder of *2Restore: Healing Church Wounds*

"The Beatles were right: *all you need is love*. Their diagnosis was timeless, but the advice of culture—both then and now—won't cure the deficiency. Only the God who is love can be the source of the ultimate solution, and in *Love*

Works Chris Conlee clarifies the way to unleash God's love into the middle of life. This book can be a game-changer for people who know what they long for but need some coaching to take it to the next level!"

Bob Shank, founder and CEO
of The Master's Program

"Chris takes these two commandments and simplifies them into a powerful equation: Love God + Love People = Love Works. This book proves that equation by sharing real-life stories from many different perspectives we can all relate to. It is a practical book for making your life work."

Robert L. Mitchell, chairman
of the board, Fellowship
of Companies for Christ International

"There are books that serve as reminders and then there are books that give revelation. *Love Works* is a resource that not only equips but also empowers followers of Jesus to love like him. Liberating and life-giving, this resource will not only be for you but for everyone God calls you to divinely love!"

Ed Newton, lead pastor
of Community Bible Church,
San Antonio, TX

"The Scriptures are clear: 'And now these three remain: faith, hope, and love. But the greatest of these is love.' There may not be any more powerful visionary ideas than these three . . . but one stands out. One fuels life change. One brings repentance. *Love*. That's why Chris wrote this book. The title says it simply and powerfully: *Love Works*. The stories and principles in this book have the capacity to change you and show you how love can work in your life. Thanks, Chris, for this important work!"

Dean Fulks, lead pastor
of Lifepoint Church

"In today's culture, where the phrase 'love wins' is a rallying cry for everything under the sun, I'm thrilled that Chris Conlee has gone far deeper with *Love Works*. Real love isn't a shallow tagline for the cause *du jour* but a sacrificial style of living that cuts directly to the meaning of life itself. Get this book. You may think you know what love is, but Chris Conlee's book will change your perspective—and potentially change your life."

Phil Cooke, PhD, writer, filmmaker,
and author of *One Big Thing:
Discovering What You Were Born to Do*

"God's universe—including your own life—strives for equilibrium. And the lever for that kind of personal congruency is love. Without love, we're out of sync. In *Love Works*, Chris Conlee takes us on an in-depth adventure, illustrating how love is the key to making life work—your life! It is the nexus providing the equilibrium God intended. Chris has left us with no shortage of actionable principles!"

Mick Ukleja, PhD, president
of LeadershipTraQ, professor, and
coauthor of *Managing the Millennials*

"If you're looking for a more authentic way to live out the love of Jesus that makes a positive, tangible difference in your world, this book is for you."

Bobby McGraw, teaching pastor
of Sugar Hill Church

LOVE**WORKS**

THE KEY TO
MAKING LIFE WORK

CHRIS**CONLEE**

BakerBooks

a division of Baker Publishing Group
Grand Rapids, Michigan

Published by Baker Books
a division of Baker Publishing Group
PO Box 6287, Grand Rapids, MI 49516-6287
www.bakerbooks.com

Printed in the United States of America

Library of Congress Cataloging-in-Publication Data
Names: Conlee, Chris, 1970– author.
Title: Love works : the key to making life work / Chris Conlee.
Description: Grand Rapids : Baker Books, 2018.
Identifiers: LCCN 2017035028 | ISBN 9780801075544 (pbk.)
Subjects: LCSH: Love—Religious aspects—Christianity.
Classification: LCC BV4639 .C5845 2018 | DDC 241/.4—dc23
LC record available at https://lccn.loc.gov/2017035028

Some names and details have been changed to protect the privacy of the individuals involved.

Author is represented by WordServe Literary Group (www
.wordserveliterary.com).

18 19 20 21 22 23 24   7 6 5 4 3 2 1

Contents

Love Works is dedicated to Karin, Mark, Annika,
and the staff and trusted teammates
of Highpoint Church.
Thank you for proving love works.
This is just the beginning.

"I pray you, show me your glory!" (Exodus 33:18 NASB)

Foreword

When Chris Conlee asked me to write a foreword for his book, *Love Works,* I was thrilled. Why? First of all, I am a raving fan of the movement Chris and his wife, Karin, have inspired with their love-based Highpoint Church. Second, Chris and I both agree that love is the key to making life work as Jesus modeled it for us.

I was struck by the simplicity and power of his equation: Love God + Love People = Love Works. What a wonderful way to summarize Jesus' rank-ordered values: (1) Love God with all your heart, soul, and mind, and (2) Love your neighbor as yourself.

In our Lead Like Jesus ministry, for which Chris and Karin have been important cheerleaders, we always say, "Love is the answer—now what is the question?"

Does love work everywhere? Chris agrees with our Lead Like Jesus philosophy that it does—whether you are engaged in organizational leadership as an executive or manager; employed as a schoolteacher, pastor, or coach; or involved in life-role leadership as a spouse, parent, child, relative, friend, or neighbor. In reality, every human being is a leader in some part of his or her life—because leadership is an influence process. Anytime you seek to influence the thinking, behavior, or development of someone in your personal or professional life, you are taking on the role of a leader. As a result, the only way to avoid leadership would be to isolate yourself from the outside world!

Chris and I both believe that leading like Jesus is love-based leadership—and that God's intention is for the primary outcome of our leadership and influence to be the demonstration of Jesus' love.

I got a letter from a New Zealander a few years ago that summed up this philosophy. He told me I am in the business of teaching people the power of love rather than the love of power. Chris is in the same business—our job as spiritual beings is to teach people the power of love rather than the love of power.

The formula Everything – Love = Nothing is not of our making. It is the irrefutable law of the kingdom of God, perfectly fulfilled by Jesus. Read *Love Works* and learn why life is about living not for ourselves but for others, by loving God and people with all our heart, soul, and mind.

Thanks, Chris, for writing this book and helping us realize that when we receive God's love, return his love, and give his love to others, it creates abundant joy in our lives. Because love works!

Ken Blanchard, coauthor of *The New One Minute Manager* and *Lead Like Jesus Revisited*

Introduction

WELL, DUH

If you've ever felt less than loved, then this book is for you.

No ordinary pool.

For miles around, that's what everyone agreed about the pool of Bethesda. Its name meant "house of outpouring," or "house of mercy," and something extraordinary happened at this strange pool in Jerusalem. What exactly?

A mysterious stirring, some called it. A holy wind. A ripple on the water caused by an unseen hand. And it wasn't the *stirring* that was the big deal, either. It was what the stirring *did* that caused such a great commotion.

All around this pool lay a great number of disabled folks, the downtrodden of ancient Jerusalem. The blind. The lame. The paralyzed. The withered. The moaning. Those with broken legs and broken arms and broken lives and broken hearts. An entire hospital of severely hurting people, all waiting for this mysterious movement of the waters. Day in, day out, all these hurting people lay by the pool.

Eager.

Expectant.

Watching.

Waiting.

They all knew exactly what they needed to see. The mysterious stirring acted like a starter's gun at a footrace. The moment the waters started to move, all manner of pandemonium broke out at the pool's edge. Shouts! Yells! Carrying. Yanking.

Then one splash. Two. Three. Four.

Only the first splash mattered because it was a big race to see who could get in the water first. Why?

Because the winner would be *healed*!

The Obvious Question—For Us Too

Got questions about the pool?

Sure.

What was behind this mysterious stirring? Why would only the first person in get healed? How would a sick person even get into the waters? How quickly could a lame man pull himself to the water's edge using only his arms? How could a blind man see the waters being stirred in the first place? How would a paralyzed person ever win a race that required moving somewhere fast? Was it even a fair system to begin with?

One man had lain at the pool for a whopping thirty-eight years. His legs and feet didn't work, and for nearly four decades he'd never been first into the pool. Oh, he'd tried. He'd watched. He'd waited. He'd moved and lunged with his hands and dragged his legs as fast as he could. He'd seen the waters stir over and over again. He'd seen success stories in other people. At first, he'd felt joy when someone made it into the pool and was healed. Hope was ahead. Surely, he'd be first next time. But it was never him.

As the months went on, the years wore on, and person after person after person made it into the pool ahead of him, disappointment set in. Then disappointment turned into discouragement. Discouragement turned into despair.

He was never first. He was never healed. He was thirty-eight years a failure. After a while, why even try anymore? Why bother?

I'm never going to be first. Oh look. The water is stirring again.

Forget it!

Then, one day, something completely different happened.

That day, a Nazarene walked by the pool of Bethesda.

A few people had already heard of this particular Nazarene. He was a relative of John the Baptizer, someone murmured, the outback mystic who wore clothes of camel's hair and ate locusts. A carpenter by trade, this Nazarene fraternized with fishermen and zealots. A tax collector or two. Even a few women of ill repute. His name was Yeshua son of Joseph. No one important enough to cause much excitement. Not yet, anyway. A bit of an odd duck, truth be told. Not even his brothers or mother understood what he was trying to do.

Yeshua seemed undaunted that day by the pool of Bethesda. When he saw a man lying there and learned

13

he'd been in that condition for thirty-eight years, Yeshua (Jesus) went over to him and asked the man what must have sounded to some like a stupid question. Well, maybe not exactly stupid, but surely the most obvious question ever asked.

"Do you want to get well?"

Well, *duh.*

The man didn't give Jesus a straightforward reply. He didn't say, "Yes. Absolutely, I want to get well." No. The man gave Jesus the answer he'd been resigned to give. It was an answer that conveyed impossibility. An answer that indicated his goal could never be achieved. An answer without hope.

"Sir," the man replied, "I have no one to help me into the pool when the water is stirred. When I am trying to get in, someone else goes down ahead of me."

Why did Jesus stop and talk to this particular man, anyway? Why single him out? What might have been different about this one man that caught Jesus' attention? Remember: around the pool lay an entire multitude of hurting people.

Maybe it was because of the answer Jesus knew the man was going to give.

"I have no one."

Think: If you were a mother or father in ancient Jerusalem, and your beloved son or daughter lay by the pool, where would you be? If your best friend lay by the pool, if one of your cherished parents lay by the pool, if your much-loved brother or sister lay by the pool, where would you be?

Of course, you'd be by that pool too!

You'd either be there yourself, or you'd have a servant or one of your family members present, or you'd do everything in your power to find someone or barter with someone to be your loved one's advocate. Somebody would be there at all times—morning, noon, night—to help your loved one get into the pool first. If you were disabled and wanted to get into the pool first, then the key to success was having others help you. And why would others help you? Because others loved you.

Yet—and this was the big clincher—this man was:

alone,

abandoned, and

hurting.

These words and more describe the man at the pool. These words describe a profound and terrible absence of love.

But let me ask you this: Have you ever felt this way?

Maybe someone gave up on you or caused you to feel like damaged goods. Maybe you desired a place or position or opportunity or relationship but you were picked last, or next to last, or not at all. Maybe you've stayed in the low position for a long time. Maybe others around you have received great opportunity, but you never have. Maybe someone let you down, or disappointed you greatly, or stopped caring about you, or held you at arm's length. Maybe someone walked away. Maybe someone overtly hurt you in some way. Maybe you've flat-out lost hope.

Welcome to the worldwide club of broken love. If you've ever felt less than loved, then this book is for you.

Why? Because this book is about a great love that's coming your way. It's about the love you receive from God, the love you give back to God, and the love you turn and give to others. It's about a perfect God loving imperfect people, and it's about us, imperfect people, learning to love better. You don't have to be perfect for love to work, and you don't have to love perfectly for love to work; you simply have to allow the One who is perfect to work his love in you and through you. The more you receive his love as an imperfect and broken person, the more moved you are to love imperfect and broken people in return. When these things happen, life falls into place. When you focus on what matters most, you live as God invites you to live: abundantly.

I can tell you this because I know what it's like to live a life that's felt broken, hurting, and alone. I've experienced great pain. I've made big mistakes. The people closest to me have let me down. I'll tell you more about my life in the pages to come. But right up front, please know this: If I can go through all this and still see love work, then love can work for you too.

It starts with this obvious question: Do you want to get well?

See, Jesus didn't leave the man at the pool of Bethesda alone in his pain. Jesus walked right over to him, looked him straight in the eyes, and met him with a heart of compassion. Jesus healed the man, and not by using any old crazy pool system either—not by using the same system that had failed the man for thirty-eight years.

Nope. Jesus healed the man because Jesus met him on the level of love, because Jesus is in the business of changing lives, and because the man responded in faith to Jesus' love. Jesus healed him because the man needed to know that someone cared about him and was willing to help him. In one glorious instant, that man went from the back of the line to the front of the line. His mourning turned into dancing. His hope was restored.

And Jesus will do this for you too.

That's what this book, *Love Works*, is all about. When we receive God's love, then love God back, then love people and help people move forward in their relationship with Jesus, then love isn't broken anymore. Love works. When love works, love does what it was designed to do. Love heals. Love rebuilds. Love restores.

My promise to you is this: we can live in this love and move forward in this love. That's why, in the pages ahead, I'm going to invite you to meet Jesus like you've never met him before. He's the One who never leaves, never forsakes, and never walks out the side door.

In a world that's full of broken love, this book will give you proof that love doesn't have to be broken. Love can do what it was designed to do: work.

If that sounds like something you'd like to know more about and make part of your life, then I invite you to keep reading.

Chris Conlee

1

When Love Hurts

For love to work, make love your priority.

Love *works?*
Yeah, right.

Love *hurts!*—that's what I'd have told you for a good many years of my life.

Let's start with my parents. Mom and Dad. My family of origin was all over the place when it came to love. When my father was just a baby, he was abandoned by his mother, my biological grandmother. She placed him in a police car when he was a year old and just walked away. Left him for the authorities to find.

My dad grew up in foster homes until he was fourteen. Then he left the foster system, set out on his own, and started working for a barbecue joint. Love wasn't working in his life, but by sheer determination he pulled himself up by his bootstraps and vowed that life would work anyway. *All I need is me*, he told himself. And from then on, he managed life by himself.

Sheer determination, as incomplete as it is, can still get you a long way in life. By the time my dad was an adult, he'd achieved a lot of life's success. Dad was a born salesman and eventually owned several franchises, including a bread business. People everywhere knew him by the nickname Bready, and everybody who knew him loved him. He was a great golfer and member of the local country club, where he was a blue collar man in a white collar world. When other men went to the country club, they drove Porsches, BMWs, and Corvettes, but Dad drove his bread truck and nobody seemed to mind. He had a warm, generous personality. A friend to all. In the suburbs where we lived, he won citizen of the year. If you were to look at him, you'd swear love was working in his life.

But I knew another side of him.

Dad had a temper like a roadside bomb. He and my mom fought all the time. I personally wrestled a gun out of my father's hands three times. Imagine yourself in a similar position. Think about looking into your dad's eyes—and they're full of rage. Imagine the worst sort of profanity flying from your father's mouth. Picture spear-like words hurled at your mom and your siblings. Imagine your dad's strong hands wrapped around a revolver, one finger on the trigger. Now imagine yourself as a teenager with your hands clawing at your father's hands. Adrenaline's coursing through your body. You're shouting. Pleading. Everybody's crying. Everybody's terrified.

My father's life was such a juxtaposition. On one hand, he was everybody's smiling friend. The guy who sold you bread.

On the other hand, he was an incredible mess.

My mother grew up with her own struggles. Her mother died when she was just five years old. Her dad remarried, but his new wife was an abusive alcoholic, and her father died when she was thirteen. She became Cinderella with a challenging stepmother. Life became a trial of anger and insults and emotional abuse. By the time my parents met and married, bless their hearts, they were basically two hurting and scarred people—dysfunctional beyond belief—who had never been nurtured by a love that works.

That was the mix of craziness I grew up in. What I saw firsthand—and then began to understand over time—was how hard it is for hurting people to love others well. I saw how healthy people help people, but hurting people hurt people—both accidentally and intentionally. If you're healthy, then thank the Lord; you're healthy because you've been loved well. Love has worked in your life. If you're unhealthy, then you haven't been loved well. Love hasn't worked in your life.

What's it like to grow up in a crazy house?

Let's start with drugs. My sister, nine years older than me, started smoking pot as a freshman in high school. Then she graduated—in a druggy sort of way—to all things harder and higher. When she was a sophomore—*poof*—she just disappeared. She ran away from home and basically dropped off everybody's radar. We had only an inkling of where she was. Any number of efforts were made to contact her and to have her contact us back. She communicated with us a bit. At least we knew she was alive. But her message was clear: if you're my family, then stay away.

Then there was perfectionism. My brother, eight years older than me, lived on the other end of the spectrum from my sister. We all called him by his nickname, Bubba, and he was our family's golden boy. A successful golfer and successful student who excelled in everything he did. He was the family's bright and shining star. But even that crashed down.

I remember the date exactly: April 20, 1981.

It started out as such a great day. My brother was a few short weeks away from graduating high school. He was a highly recruited golfer, already signed to play for Ole Miss. That day, he played in a high school golf match and shot a 64, the best round of his life. You have to realize how incredible his score was. Standard par is 72. The average golfer shoots in the 90s. Pros shoot high-to-mid 60s on a good day. I mean, my brother was a rising star, the Tiger Woods of his day.

He was pumped up. He was playing the best golf of his life. Everything was falling into place for an incredible college career. He drove toward where he knew my dad and I were working to tell us about his round. At least, that's how we've come to piece together the story today.

Me? I remember the day like a nightmare.

Dad and I were at the gas station, filling up his bread truck. I heard a train in the distance but that sound barely registered in my mind. What did register was a screech and a thud, the horrible sound of metal colliding with metal. I remember heading around the corner to see the accident, but my dad grabbed my shoulders and yelled: "Get in the truck! I don't want you to see!"

It wasn't until we drove home and saw three police cars parked in our driveway that we learned whose car had been involved in the wreck. Bubba's. I'll never forget the devastation of that moment. Before Bubba's death, our family was broken but still together. After Bubba's death, our family was shattered and separated. We lost far more than Bubba; we lost one another. We didn't grieve together as a family. We isolated ourselves. We self-medicated. We compartmentalized our feelings. We tried to survive as individuals.

That was my family's experience with love.

Two horribly broken parents.

A sister on drugs who was missing.

A shining-star brother who was killed one month before graduation day.

And me. A guy who felt it all.

I was ten years old when my brother died. What I felt so keenly then was an immense hurt in my soul. Love was not working in our family as a whole.

And not only was love not working . . .

Love hurt like hell.

When Love Begins to Work

See, before love could start to work in my life, I needed to meet love first. And I discovered that love wasn't a concept or a theory or a happy story from the movies.

Love was a Person named Jesus.

As a kid, if asked if I knew Jesus, I'd probably mumble, "Yeah, sure." I was an American after all, and all Americans are Christians—aren't they? At least, that's what my parents believed. For many years, my parents were Christians in name only. We darkened the door of the church on Christmas and Easter, but that was it. There was no real following of Jesus in any of our lives. No healing. No wholeness. No love, joy, or peace.

When I was fifteen, I went to a youth camp in Destin, Florida, where I heard the good news laid out for me simply: God is amazing. He's better than the best thing we could ever imagine. And God wants to have a relationship with us. Yet all people have sinned and fallen short of the glory of God. Even me. I was separated from God because of my sin. The wages of sin are death—not physical death, but spiritual death. Thanks to my sin, I was separated from real love. Fortunately, Jesus was the bridge between God and me.

So I made the decision right then and there at that youth camp. I trusted Jesus as my Lord and Savior. My life was still a mess in many ways, but a good and noble seed was planted deep in the soil of my heart. God's love took root there, and God's love began to work on my hurt.

One day that same year, the phone rang. It was the pastor at the Baptist church we attended on and off. They'd been doing some cleaning and found my brother's Bible. Did we want it?

Remember, this was five years after he'd died.

My parents weren't home at the time. I had a little motorbike, so I kicked its engine to life, puttered up to the church, and got the Bible. I remember its weight. The sleekness of the cover. I pictured my brother reading it. In the sanctuary I plunked myself down on the back pew, and the Bible flopped open to Colossians 3:2. A creased page. A star was inked in the margin, and written beside it, in my brother's handwriting, was "My life verse."

Set your minds on things that are above, not on things that are on earth. (ESV)

I read those words slowly. I read them twice. Three times. Four. What did that mean—to set my mind on things above? I didn't know all what it meant, but it was like a light went on in my soul. My brother's life verse became my life verse too. And from that moment on—slowly yet deliberately—I chose to live by that verse. In the process, God found me, protected me, provided for me, and guided me forward in his grace. Throughout the following years, God put person after person into my life who showed me that love works. Jesus invited me into his better story. When it came to my spiritual growth, I didn't walk perfectly, but I walked with progress.

Today, some thirty years later, my mind is still set on things above and my life is deeply immersed in the world of ministering to hurting people. I can clearly see when love doesn't work in people's lives because I've been there myself. I've committed my life to solving the problem of love not working. I'm driven by this goal because I've lived in both worlds. I've seen love not work and I've seen how miserable life is then. And I've seen love work and I know how great life can be too.

That's how I want to start this book. Simply by identifying with your pain. If you're in a place of big hurt right now, then, absolutely, please know I can feel what that's like along with you. Or maybe you wouldn't exactly classify your life as a place of "big" hurt, but you know some things aren't the way you'd like them to be. Pain is a scale we're all on to one degree or another. You know there's got to be more to life than what you're experiencing today.

Here are the facts. I've personally seen both sides of the equation: a love that's broken and a love that works. In my life, I've been through all levels of heartbreak and pain, and I'm still here to tell you that the only thing that works is love. The only reason I'm a victor instead of a victim is because I chose to believe and experienced that love still works. Walk through this book with me and see how God can prove that love works in your life too.

All of us can point to times and situations in our lives when love has felt like it wasn't working. Maybe a relationship didn't work out as we'd hoped. A friendship turned sour. Maybe someone who we wished would speak words of affirmation to us spoke words of belittlement instead. Maybe a person who meant a great deal to us let us down, or backed away, or didn't show up, or didn't come through. A relationship that was supposed to be great didn't turn out to be great at all.

Can you picture such a situation in your life? The bottom line is the same: we wanted love but instead received hurt.

What do we do, then? How do we proceed? Is there a way for love to be fixed again?

Instead of love being broken, how can love work?

The Crux of Every Problem

Maybe this is a completely new idea to you—that love doesn't need to be broken. Let me explain how the premise for this book began. Several years back, I led the leadership team at our church through an intense time of brainstorming and research. We asked ourselves this question: What's the biggest problem people deal with today? What's the one big thing everybody wrestles with? We knew if this one big problem was solved, it would solve a ton of secondary problems too.

The big problem that emerged was *broken love.* Our greatest hurts and problems occur when love doesn't work.

Love is so central to how we live. Every movie has a plot twist about love. Every novel. Every song on the radio. Love surrounds our lives because we all long for love. When we talk about love, we mean having affection for another person. Respect. Consideration. Honor. Service. Gratitude. Kindness. Acting with integrity and thoughtfulness toward each other. It's reciprocal: we love people, and they love us back. We all long for deep, personal attachments. With love in our lives, we set goals. We find security and significance. We have hope and go forward. We all want love.

Ask yourself these questions:

What would my life be like without love?

Is there anything better than love? Any amount of money, any possession, any pleasure, any activity, any priority? (If you think so, imagine having all of those things without anyone to share them with.)

If love isn't the answer, then what else is?

Think about all the benefits of love. With love, we smile more. We hug more, we kiss more, we laugh more—we feel wanted and needed and safe and powerful and helpful and important and inspired.

With love, people are sheltered and fed and cared for.

With love, people are forgiven and freed.

With love, marriages stay together. Families stay together. Children are safe and secure, healthy and happy.

Love is clearly the answer.

Yet problems abound in this world. We saw as a leadership team that the very thing we long for often *isn't* working the way it's supposed to. We can basically trace every problem to love being broken. What kinds of bad things happen when love doesn't work?

> If love doesn't work, we're lonely.
>
> If love doesn't work, we start trying to meet the need for love in other ways.
>
> If love doesn't work, we're isolated and we turn to harmful substances or things that fill the void.
>
> If love doesn't work, we're more anxious and angry. We're sadder. We're disheartened. We're annoyed. We're bitter.
>
> If love doesn't work, we have more tension, trauma, and stress. We cry more often. We have more health problems. We feel miserable. We lose direction. We lose hope.

Let's face it: just like healthy love is full of blessings, broken love is full of consequences. One of those consequences is that broken love begets broken love. Our problem is not simply that love isn't there. It's that love *is* there but it's damaged; someone who is supposed to love us is actually causing us pain.

> Maybe we told a person off and burned a relational bridge. Or they us.
>
> Maybe the idea of a family reunion makes our stomach quake.

Maybe every relationship we've ever been in has ended badly.

Maybe we crossed the line into legal territory and sued a person. Or they us.

Maybe we quit a job when we didn't need to, or broke up a marriage, or severed relational ties when they shouldn't have been severed, or stormed off in a huff, or don't call a friend anymore, or can't stand the thought of a specific person anymore, or get nervous when a person is merely named, or can't stand to see a certain person around town. Or they us.

Maybe, when we realized love wasn't working, we hung our heads and felt defeated and abandoned. Or we crawled into bed and put the covers over our heads—maybe literally, maybe figuratively. We didn't fight the situation. We ran. We cowered. We disappeared.

We knew love was broken, so we just let love be broken. In our sorrow and pain and despair, we wept. Love hurt, and we desperately longed for it to feel better.

What do we do, then? Please tell us there's a solution for broken love!

The Only Solution

Here's the good news: love can work.

Giving evidence to this became our goal as a leadership team. We wanted to learn everything we could about love and then show people love doesn't need to be broken, so their lives could be better too. We started studying what real love is. We examined case studies of love in action.

We developed principles we could all live by. We started applying these principles to real life situations.

We found that far too many churches emphasize head knowledge over everything else. It's certainly not wrong to know a lot about the Bible, but that's not God's primary calling on anyone's life. The primary call is always to love God while loving other people. First Corinthians 13 is clear about this. We can have all sorts of amazing gifts and do all sorts of amazing things in the name of Jesus, but if loving people isn't at the top of our list, then everything else is worthless. True spiritual maturity isn't measured by knowledge but by relationship.

Think about it this way: Have you ever noticed how we tend to gloss over familiar Bible passages? Maybe we memorized a particular verse as a kid or we were taught it in Sunday school. Maybe we saw the verse on TV when a quarterback painted it in black ink under his eyes. When verses become too familiar, we have a tendency to ignore them. But what if we were to see those familiar verses in a new light? What if we saw a truth not only as *head* knowledge—but as *heart* knowledge too?

> *True spiritual maturity isn't measured by knowledge but by relationship.*

What I mean is that it's easy to know a truth in our minds. Sure, we see a truth and give mental acquiescence to it. But do we also live it out? Have we ingested the truth into our hearts so it's become part of us in the way we live our lives every day? Have we caught not only the informational part of the verse, but the relational aspect of it too?

Here's a familiar verse:

For God so loved the world, that he gave his only Son, that whoever believes in him should not perish but have eternal life. (John 3:16 ESV)

How many times have you heard that rattled off? But wait. Look more closely.

God loves you and me and the whole world. He loves us in all of our pains, all of our hurts, all of our insecurities, all of our imperfections, and all of our attempts to be better than we actually are. God so loved the world that he gave what was most important to him: Jesus, his Son. Why? So whoever believes in him won't be separated from God by sin but would have eternal life. A life of abundance. A better story.

So, that's John 3:16. But John wrote more than one book in the Bible. Here's the harder question: What does 1 John 3:16 say? (Did you catch the "*First*" John?)

This is how we know what love is: Jesus Christ laid down his life for us. And we ought to lay down our lives for our brothers and sisters.

Wow, what a tremendous truth! Let's unpack that verse not only in our minds, but in our hearts too.

"This is how we know what love is: Jesus Christ laid down his life for us." Good. We've heard that already. That's a summary of the gospel, a reminder of John 3:16.

Then John goes on to say, "And we ought to lay down our lives for our brothers and sisters." That's the new truth from John. In light of this verse, what are we called to do?

Jesus laid down his life for us, and we in turn ought to lay down our lives for others. Who, specifically? Our spouse. Our children. Our friends. Our coworkers. Our neighbors.

Even the people we don't get along with so well. Developing love for others is our ministry, our calling. Thanks to God's incredible love for us, we are to receive the love of Jesus, then return his love back to God, then love others with his love.

Read 1 John 3:16 one more time and notice all the relational words in the verse. By "relational" words, I mean all the words that relate to us as people.

> This is how **WE** know what love is: Jesus Christ laid down his life for **US**. And **WE** ought to lay down **OUR** lives for **OUR BROTHERS** and **SISTERS**.

These are the words that move us from informational to relational. By using both head knowledge *and* heart knowledge, we broaden the paradigm of what it means to be Christians. We follow Jesus because there's abundant life promised for us. Yes. We follow Jesus because our lives bring glory and fame to God. Yes. We follow Jesus because God has a wonderful plan for our lives. Yes.

And then we also follow Jesus so we can give love away.

What passages such as 1 John 3:16 indicate is that God's love can flow through us. The abundance is in the giving. Certainly, there's joy in receiving God's love, but the fullness of joy comes in giving God's love. God's love is about us—but it's always about so much more than us. It's about God, us, and others. That's the only way God's love works—in its fullness. This is the ministry Jesus calls us to. We're to live lives of *total* love. When we give love away, our love flows to others and benefits them. It also flows back to us and benefits us. The benefit goes both ways.

When we give love:

people are forgiven,

people are freed,

people are encouraged,

people are helped,

we smile more than we frown,

we laugh more than we cry,

we're happy more than we're sad, and

we exchange our problems for peace.

Four Big Commandments in a Nutshell

So, how does love work? How does Jesus invite us to live a life of love?

It's not hard.

Jesus calls us to live by the four big commandments of love: the Great Commandment, the Golden Rule, the New Commandment, and the Great Commission. Jesus spoke the words of these commandments for all of his disciples—not just to the twelve who followed him closely, but for us today too.

Let's look at each one, then put them all together.

- *The Great Commandment* (Matt. 22:37–39). "'Love the Lord your God with all your heart and with all your soul and with all your mind.' This is the first and greatest commandment. And the second is like it: 'Love your neighbor as yourself.'"
- *The Golden Rule* (Matt. 7:12). "Do to others what you would have them do to you."

- *The New Commandment* (John 13:34). "A new command I give you: Love one another. As I have loved you, so you must love one another."
- *The Great Commission* (Matt. 28:18–20). "All authority in heaven and on earth has been given to me. Therefore go and make disciples of all nations, baptizing them in the name of the Father and of the Son and of the Holy Spirit, and teaching them to obey everything I have commanded you. And surely I am with you always, to the very end of the age."

Here's what happens when we merge the four together. Remember, the commandments aren't merely informational. They're relational too. Sure, God wants us to know things, but mostly he wants us to live out what we know. The point of spiritual maturity is never that we fill our heads with facts. It's that we live a life of love. So, what if we woke up every single day and lived out these four commandments relationally? The four can be summed up like this:

> Receive his love.
> Return his love.
> Give his love.

See, something resonates so deeply within us when we see the goodness of God through what he calls us to do. We serve a God who is holy and sovereign, who wraps his character and response to us in love. We receive the love God has for us. We love God back. Then we turn and love other people. When we do this, then love works.

Hey, when we do this, then *life* works. How do we know? Let me conclude this chapter by telling you Byron's story. He's one of the many people who has proved love works.

Byron's New Tattoo

At first, Byron couldn't believe I was a pastor.

Byron and I were both assistant coaches on our sons' football team, and his disbelief wasn't because I yelled a lot or used foul language on the field. (Well, actually I yelled a lot, but only because I'm passionate about football!) No, Byron had a hard time believing I was a pastor because I intentionally don't broadcast my profession. People wonder if they should treat a pastor differently or candycoat their speech or stop being real. So I kept quiet on the field. Except when I was cheering for our team!

One day after practice, we were walking to our cars and Byron asked me, "Conlee, what do you do for a living?"

I told him I was a pastor, and he said, "No, seriously. Really? You're the guy who speaks on Sunday?" And I said, "Yeah, that's me. Trust me, I have a hard time believing it too." He said, "Well, I've got to check this out." I said, "Definitely, I'd love for you to come this Sunday. It's a unique place, not your normal church; I'd love to hear your thoughts." So he did, and our friendship entered a new level.

It's funny: When people start going to church, they begin to glimpse a better story. They encounter Jesus through the words of Scripture and the actions of people. They see God loves them. They see how Jesus invites them to love others as a reflection of his greater love. They see how Jesus offers us the promise of an abundant life.

Byron was no exception. He was going through a divorce at the time, an understandably difficult season in anyone's life. Fortunately, Byron decided to follow Jesus, and then Byron's son followed Jesus. Father and son were baptized at our church. We all became good friends. Byron and I began meeting regularly so we could talk about Jesus more and explore how Byron could move forward in his faith and work through his divorce. We found we had a lot to talk about; my life was far from perfect, and Byron's life was far from perfect. Picture two imperfect people having breakfast each week at Chick-Fil-A. That was us.

I wish I could tell you that as soon as Byron began following Jesus his life became problem-free and his marriage was healed. But no, that didn't happen. It's true that everything changed for the better in terms of Byron's standing before a righteous and holy God. Byron had faith, hope, and love because of Jesus. Byron found forgiveness and freedom because of Jesus. But Jesus never promises any of us a problem-free life. And, unfortunately, Byron's marriage was not repaired.

Divorce is tricky. I've never experienced divorce personally, but I've seen it play out in a lot of lives. One big dynamic in a divorce is that two people who were once in love with each other aren't anymore. Love was working for them once, but now love isn't working. Two people are forced to unravel a relationship that was never meant to be unraveled.

To make matters more difficult for Byron, his ex-wife planned to move from Memphis to Houston, a ten-hour drive away, and take their son with her. Byron was crushed. He was a good father and loved his son dearly. The broken love between Byron and his wife was prompting an additional hurt in Byron's life—the very real possibility he wouldn't be involved in his son's life on a day-to-day basis. Faced with that thought, Byron confided in me that he felt his whole world was falling apart.

At the time of the divorce, my son and Byron's son were both the same age: nine years old. I personally knew how important it is in a young boy's life to have his father around. When Byron first told me his ex-wife was moving ten hours away to Houston, this is what I said to Byron:

"You need to move too."

Period.

It wasn't an order. That's not how I do business as a friend or pastor. It was an insistence born from love and concern for my friend. I knew Byron could not be separated from his son by so much distance for so long at a time in this season of life. Byron needed to do whatever it took to move to Houston so he could spend the next nine years with the boy he cared so deeply about. If he did, then that would lay the foundation for having a relationship with his son for the rest of his life. But if he didn't move, he'd become a part-time father. His relationship with his son would become that much more challenging. I said, "In order for love to work, you need to do whatever it takes to overcome this obstacle in your relationship with him."

Byron knew the advice was right, but he was naturally concerned about his career and all the logistics involved. A move of that distance wouldn't be easy. He'd need to find another job, and in your forties it's difficult to find positions with comparable pay and upward opportunities. He hated the thought of his ex-wife "winning" (his words). He asked, "Why is this move so much more complicated and costly for me? This is unfair."

But this was not about winning or losing. This was about loving his son.

So Byron made plans.

On his last day in Memphis, Byron came to see me. He thanked me for introducing him to Jesus and for being his friend. Everything that had happened in Byron's spiritual life began with friendship and was sustained by friendship. (It's possible that friendship might be the most undervalued aspect of anyone's spiritual journey, for friendship paves the way for love to work.)

Highpoint Church, where I pastor, has a logo that carries great symbolism, and I regularly explain this logo to all our people. It's an arrow within a circle. The arrow points up, but it does so at an angle, not straight up. It means we are always orienting our lives Godward. Yet we make progress imperfectly, at an angle. Thanks to the grace of Jesus, we make progress, anyway.

Byron rolled up his sleeve. On his upper arm, he showed me a new tattoo: the angled arrow within the circle. "Why did I get this?" he said. "Because you've shown me that love works." Wow—that was a tear-filled, speechless moment.

The move proved difficult. Byron looked for a job in Houston but found nothing. A month went by and still no job. Three months. Six months. Nine months. Eighteen months. Still no job. Finally, he found a job in Austin, an hour and a half away from Houston. He asked me if he should take the job. I told him yes; the job wasn't ideal, but the drive-time between Austin and Houston was a whole lot shorter than Memphis to Houston. He could still meet with his son every weekend and achieve the relational goals important to him. Byron took the job.

For two years, Byron commuted from Austin to Houston every weekend, being a faithful father to his son. We talked on the phone a lot. Love was working, he said. He and his son were staying close.

Byron stayed close to Jesus too, letting the love of Christ wash through his life and change his thoughts, words, and actions. He saw how Jesus invited him to commit himself to excellence, and pretty soon Byron became the number-one salesman at his new company. He was able to relocate to Houston and go from being a weekend dad to a daily dad. He bought a house in the same neighborhood as his ex-wife, and for the next six years until Byron's son graduated, he and his son lived less than one mile away from each other.

The happy ending to this story is that today, nine-plus years after the divorce, Byron and his wife have a good working relationship as coparents. Their son is flourishing in the love of both parents and was recently awarded a scholarship to play baseball in college. Byron would tell you that the decision to prioritize love was an incredibly important decision for him to make. Nine years later, he can't imagine not making that decision. What would he have missed if he wasn't committed to doing the work necessary to prove love works? Previously, Byron's life was filled with hurt because love was broken. But Jesus led Byron to prioritize love over everything else, and Byron learned how to make love work.

What Matters Most in Life?

That's what this book is all about: the one solution to all your problems. Brokenness doesn't need to be the end of your story. Love can work regardless of your circumstances, regardless of your pain and disappointment.

And love doesn't need to be perfect to work, either. We're all travelers on this journey. We all walk by faith in grace.

In front of you and me today is a massive call to be great at what matters most: to receive God's love in our hearts. To love God with all our heart, soul, mind, and strength. Then to let the love of God flow through us so we love other people like Christ loves us. This is the singular message of this book—and I hope it comes through loud and clear: *love works*.

Love can work regardless of your circumstances, regardless of your pain and disappointment.

Do you want a life that makes sense? Do you want more peace and joy? Do you want to live the abundant life that Christ promises us? The information in the pages ahead is simple yet biblically profound. I'm going to show you what we learned as a team: how to have a sustainable and livable expression of love. When you live out this love, the benefit comes back to you. You'll have more peace, more patience, more kindness, more gentleness, more goodness, more faithfulness, and more self-control. And more. Against these things, there is no law (Gal. 5:22–23), and there are absolutely no drawbacks, complications, penalties, or side effects to living this way.

But there can be some challenges to this. And one of the challenges is that we need to redefine what success in life looks like.

If you'd like to watch Byron tell his story, go to ChrisConlee.net.

2

Of Babies
and Business Cards

Life is messy, but love conquers the mess.

Pick one word to describe the Peterson family and I'd say *close*. They were close with each other and close to the church—Mom, Dad, and their four tall and beautiful girls.

Pick two words and I'd say *wholehearted* and *wholesome*. Mom and Dad raised their girls with a faithful foundation, constantly encouraging them to study the Bible, pray, memorize Scripture, and know Jesus more.

Pick three words and I'd say *perfect Hallmark family*. I mean, this family was the all-American definition of security, safety, and sentimentality. Their oldest daughter, Chelsea, always seemed particularly solid while growing up. Ask her today, as an adult, and she'll tell you her sisters as teens had "wilder" personalities than she ever did (for the Peterson family, I think "wilder" meant ordering stuffed-crust pizza on Friday nights). But Chelsea was the rule-follower in the family, the one who always earned good grades, the mild-mannered firstborn who kept the other siblings in line.

Chelsea also describes how the pledge to remain sexually pure was something her parents instilled in her and her sisters. "God has something better for you" was a message they often heard. And Chelsea kept that vow all through high school.

But in college, things began to unravel. Her dad got a job in another state. Chelsea was enrolled at the University of Memphis at the time, so her parents moved to New Jersey while she stayed put. Chelsea describes now how the faith that had seemed so rock solid was really the faith of her parents only. She was riding their coattails and had yet to develop a real faith of her own. Chelsea started to step over the line and live in the world. She didn't stay plugged into church. She tried to sugarcoat her behavior, telling people she was doing okay if they asked, but in reality she was living a conflicted life. Truly, it was a dark time for her.

She met a young man named Will her senior year of college. He was heading toward medical school. They started dating. Before long, Chelsea was pregnant.

"I was absolutely paralyzed by the news," Chelsea says. "Just terrified and numb. Will was supportive, but this was the first time in my life I ever felt truly alone. I'd been trying to hide who I was for so long, but the pregnancy caused me to take a serious look in the mirror at who I'd become. I had no idea what to do. It felt debilitating to let my parents down like this. I didn't tell them for an entire month."

When Chelsea finally told her parents, they expressed their unconditional love for her, yet they were also genuinely grieved. Their trust had been eroded. They wanted the best for their daughter, but knew that some difficult choices now needed to be made. It proved a difficult time for the entire family. Chelsea's dad had been very successful throughout the years, but he'd lost his job in the 2008 recession and was having trouble finding work in the new economy. Chelsea's mom worked long hours as a nurse. Money was tight, and the parents and younger daughters lived in a cramped apartment in New Jersey, quite different from their previous lifestyle.

For Chelsea and Will, the natural choice was to get married—as soon as possible. Six weeks after Chelsea found out she was pregnant, Will proposed. Chelsea said yes, but right from the start things turned sour. They barely knew each other. Everything was too fast, too soon. Will said he believed in God, and he and Chelsea had talked about spiritual matters once or twice, but that was it. The plan to get married seemed more about trying to fix the pregnancy than about uniting their lives in real and lasting love.

Chelsea came to me for counsel and to see if I'd perform the wedding. I asked Chelsea some pointed questions about where Will was in his faith, and from the answers she gave, it was clear Will didn't have a real relationship with Jesus. He was a "good guy" and perhaps called himself a Christian, but he wasn't close to being the spiritual leader he needed to be. He wasn't prepared to take on this role in his new married life and didn't even want to go to church with Chelsea. When it came to her own faith, Chelsea was working through a lot too. She says, "I just sat there in that first meeting and thought, 'Oh my word, Will's not a believer, and I don't even know what I am anymore.'"

The counsel I gave Chelsea was this: just because they'd made one bad decision (getting pregnant before marriage) didn't mean they needed to make a second bad decision (getting married without having a solid foundation of love). My wife, Karin, and I have seen too many situations where people marry for the wrong reasons, and those marriages seldom work out as hoped. So I counseled them to slow down so they could discern if marriage was the right solution. (They could still be parents without being married, although this wasn't an ideal solution, either.) At the very least, they should wait thirty days to think and pray through matters and have the hard conversations that needed to be had. A decision of this magnitude and importance needed to be based on unified values. Ultimately, I put the decision back in their laps. If they felt that God was leading them to be married, then I'd perform the ceremony.

That meeting proved pivotal. Chelsea described how she got in her car after the meeting and had a meltdown. She knew the façade she was putting up was not a fix. Later, she met up with Will and told him she loved him but thought it best to put wedding plans on hold, seek God, and figure out his best plans for the future. Will was a bit confused but he agreed to wait.

Chelsea had just graduated from university. She and Will had talked about moving in together, but Chelsea didn't want to make another inevitable bad choice. She moved in with her parents in New Jersey. One month turned into two months. Three months. Five. Will and Chelsea spent their time away from each other thinking, talking, and praying.

Or at least Chelsea did. Life back in New Jersey wasn't easy for the Peterson family as a whole. Chelsea's mom was worn out. Her dad was still without a job. The family was out of money. New and unfamiliar tensions arose.

In the meantime, a couple of Will's buddies started pouring into him spiritually, talking to him about Jesus and taking him to church. Previously, he'd been wounded by a Christian friend who'd done him wrong, and he felt hurt by Chelsea for putting the wedding plans on hold. But gradually, he began to understand about forgiveness for his friend and about why Chelsea had left and found it necessary to sort things through.

They waited; then, with one month to go before the baby was born, Will phoned Chelsea and said, "The next time we're together, I want us to get married." Chelsea agreed. She didn't care about having her dream wedding anymore. She knew it would be nothing close. Everything wasn't perfect in her relationship with Will, but their ties were getting stronger. They made plans just to go down to the courthouse and tie the knot. Maybe host a very small dinner afterward. Absolutely nothing fancy. A date was set.

Chelsea asked her sister, Sarah, to travel down to Memphis with her and stay with her for a couple of weeks until the wedding date. Sarah was a real prayer warrior who still dreamed big for her sister, and she began to pray boldly that God would take care of every detail of the wedding. But it was still an uphill battle. Cash was so tight for the Petersons that the rest of the family couldn't even afford to travel to Memphis for the wedding. Chelsea was crushed. Her family had always been so close. She still felt ashamed of the decisions she'd made. "I felt like a joke," Chelsea told me. "I was big as a house and supposed to be married. I said, 'God isn't going to bless this.'"

That's where I want to stop this story for now—with restoration still feeling like it's a long way off. Why stop here? Because a lot of us can relate to this feeling—either with something we're going through or with something a friend is going through. Something difficult has happened, and life has not worked out as planned. We are coming back to God, starting to make our faith our own and starting to walk more closely with him, but it's still a rollercoaster and some days are better than others. Or perhaps we've walked with the Lord for a while now but we've been through some sort of chaotic experience—perhaps caused by our own sin or the sin of others. We need to contend with life's messiness and it takes a while for restoration to seem full and complete.

Ultimately, we're still chewing on a question—does love actually work? We are taking Romans 8:28 and posing it as a query: we want to know if all things truly will work together for good for those who love God.

A Love of Action

When Chelsea got pregnant, love wasn't working. Chelsea and Will had based their relationship on premarital sex, and an unplanned pregnancy wasn't going to create the necessary foundation for a successful relationship. Like many people, Chelsea had hoped for a storybook wedding someday, a beautiful marriage, blessed with the trust and support of her parents. But because of the eroded trust and her parents' financial complications, nothing was working out the way Chelsea had hoped. The situation was heading toward restoration. But restoration hadn't fully arrived yet.

That's where love needs to step in and roll up its sleeves. Chelsea's situation was ripe for what I call "redefining excellence"—one of the foundational principles of this book. When we redefine something, we give it a new framework; we change our perspective. Maybe we've always defined excellence one way but now we need to see excellence in a different light. In Christ's light. The responsibility for redefining excellence didn't only rest with Will and Chelsea—it rested on the shoulders of all of us who were called to love them and be involved in their lives. Together, how could we make love work?

Part of the solution emerges when we focus on giving back, on loving other people. Remember the formula for abundant living we talked about in the first chapter? The plan is a distillation of the Great Commandment, the Golden Rule, the New Commandment, and the Great Commission. It's straightforward: we receive love from God and we return love to God, and then it's not complete until we give his love away to others.

Too often we focus on receiving love only. We might even express our love back to God in the form of worship and prayer. But we miss the third component: giving to others. And giving makes a lot of sense for us. More smiling happens when we give love away. When we give to others, we have more peace, joy, laughter, and abundance. Everybody wants that.

Those four big commandments of God aren't merely informational, either. They're relational. God wants us to know things, and he wants us to live out what we know. It's so important that we grasp this relational component of love that I emphasize it again. Life throws any number of problems and questions in our way, like what happened to Chelsea and Will, and the "answer" to life is always Jesus. But Jesus, strangely enough, is not the "answer." Does that sound like heresy to you? Hang on before you burn this book! The catch is that Jesus is a person. We can't have a relationship with an *answer* but we can have a relationship with a *person*, with Jesus. See the difference?

Think of it this way. I have a friend, I'll call him Myles, who had a son with a woman and tried to connect with her and the baby but wasn't able to make it work. He paid child support over the years but that was the extent of his relationship with his son. Then Myles got saved and started following Jesus, and he went to look for the woman and his son, wondering if he could connect. This time, the mom said yes. So Myles took the boy, who was now twelve years old, out to dinner, and during that dinner Myles apologized for not being part of the boy's life.

The boy started crying and said, "I'm not crying because I'm upset with you."

"Then what are the tears about?" Myles asked.

"For the longest time, I've seen my older brother go over to his dad's house," the boy said, "and I've always wondered what it was like to have a dad and go to his house. Now I'm just sitting here in disbelief that I finally have a dad."

The next morning, the mother called Myles and said, "I hope you know how much this means that you've entered your son's life. I went into our boy's room and found him asleep with your business card in his hand."

The next day, Myles bought the boy some basketball shoes, played some hoops with him at our church's gym, and went to a game with him later that evening. When I saw the boy, he was walking with his head held high, his shoulders back, proud that he had a dad.

That's the difference between an "answer" and a "relationship." If someone were to ask the boy if he had a biological father, the boy always knew the "answer"—yes. But the answer by itself felt cold, because it was head knowledge only. When the boy actually knew who his father was, when his father took him out to dinner, bought him shoes, played basketball with him, and took him to a game—that's when a real relationship began. And the relationship was wonderful—it gave the boy identity and security, even hope. The boy is a bit short for his age, but Myles is more than six feet tall. So the boy could look at his dad with new hope of who he'd become.

Jesus is like this with us. He is not merely the answer to life's questions. He is who we belong to. In Jesus we find our identity, purpose, and peace. Yes, Jesus is our answer, but he's far more than our answer. Jesus is "God with us" (Matt. 1:23). He's not a principle to agree or disagree with. He's a Person to get to know.

> *He's not a principle to agree or disagree with. He's a Person to get to know.*

So, let's start putting these various components together. For love to work, we know we need a relationship with Jesus and we can't merely receive love— we have to receive it from God, return it to God, and then give it away to others too. But how do we actually do that? Is love merely a feeling that we impose on other people? Do we just walk around telling people we love them?

Here's the crux of the question: How do we actually give love away to other people?

The answer is "with action." We move. We act. We do. We work for other people out of the compassion Christ creates in us. First John 3:18 is key: "Dear children, let us not love with words or speech but with actions and in truth." If we merely pay lip service to the idea of loving other people, we won't get anywhere. Real love is expressed relationally—through actions and in truth. To truly love other people we must do something about it. We need to punch our ticket and get to work. Our actions prove that love exists, and everything we want in life is found in love.

Three Action Plans

If you've ever been to a wedding ceremony, then you've undoubtedly heard 1 Corinthians 13 being read. The passage is all about love, and it's one of the most famous passages in the Bible.

But the passage doesn't specifically refer to marital love. Not in the larger context. The passage is sandwiched between two other chapters—1 Corinthians 12 and 14—and both of those chapters are all about gifting and service. So, the Bible's greatest chapter about love isn't given in the context of marriage (although the chapter can be applied to that). It's actually given in the context of using our giftedness for serving others and building others up. That's what we're talking about in this chapter. For love to work, we must work.

Here's how 1 Corinthians 13 stacks up. Paul's definition of love involves our behavior and our actions, not merely our intentions and speech. Anything short of action is simply aspiration, and that's not the full experience of love. A loveless person produces nothing and gains nothing. God's commandment for us isn't merely that we'd know more about love—it's that we'd actually love more. In sixteen verses, we find eight descriptions of what love *is* and eight descriptions of what love *isn't*.

Let's put those descriptions into three action plans for us.

1. For love to work, love must guide everything we do.

If I speak in the tongues of men or of angels, but do not have love, I am only a resounding gong or a clanging cymbal. If I have the gift of prophecy and can fathom all mysteries and all knowledge, and if I have a faith that can move mountains, but do not have love, I am nothing. If I give all I possess to the poor and give over my body to hardship that I may boast, but do not have love, I gain nothing. (1 Cor. 13:1–3)

Tragedy colors these first three verses: a picture of God-followers making a lot of noise but accomplishing nothing. Sadly, this is what characterizes much of the church today. We make too much noise and not enough music. We pound gongs and beat cymbals and the problem is mostly of our own making. We reap what we have sown. We have become known as critical people, Christians who boycott businesses and criticize causes we don't agree with. The remedy is compassion in action. Love must guide all our actions—our

> *God's commandment for us isn't merely that we'd know more about love—it's that we'd actually love more.*

conversations, our voting, our posts on social media, our public personas, the way we handle Scripture, our acts of faith, and any acts of service and justice. If we lead with love, then our noise will be turned into beautiful song.

It's easy to be noisy. We can have a lot of good things going for us—power, knowledge, and faith (all extraordinary). But if we don't have love, then all the rest is worth nothing. Nada. Zero. Zip. Zilch. That's what the text says. Apart from love, there are *zero* good works. The loveless person produces nothing, gains nothing, and is nothing.

By contrast, in 1 John 4:8 we read that "God is love," and that's our true identity. Our Father's identity is love, so as his children, our identity is also love. When we don't love, we have lost our identity. We disconnect from the Father.

If we have no identity in Christ, then our identity becomes based on our performance. We might build big ministries or serve until our fingers are worn to the bone or give lots of money to God, but if we don't have love, then it's all worthless. We see pastors and spiritual leaders who lead out of their competency. They expend great amounts of energy and resources for the sake of Jesus and end up burning out or falling away. Why? Because oftentimes their competency is more developed than their character. They lead with competency, not the love of Christ.

Love must guide everything we do.

2. For love to work, it must build people up instead of tear people down.

Love is patient, love is kind. It does not envy, it does not boast, it is not proud. It does not dishonor others, it is not self-seeking, it is not easily angered, it keeps no record of wrongs. Love does not delight in evil but rejoices with the truth. It always protects, always trusts, always hopes, always perseveres. (1 Cor. 13:4–7)

What does love look like, or not look like? At the top of the list, love is patient and kind. For love to work, we must act without complaint, without losing our temper, and without showing irritation. The converse is equally true. If we *don't* want love to work, then we boast, we're wrongfully proud of what we can do, we dishonor others, we seek our own interests, we're easily angered, and we keep records of wrongs.

If we want to love someone, then we protect this person, trust this person, hope for good things for this person, and keep loving this person despite difficult times. Conversely, if we want love to hurt instead of heal, then we expose this person to danger without protection, we don't trust this person, we have no hope for this person, and we abandon ship at the first sign of trouble.

So, love must guide everything, and love must build people up instead of tear people down.

3. For love to work, it must be a lasting love.

Love never fails. But where there are prophecies, they will cease; where there are tongues, they will be stilled; where there is knowledge, it will pass away. For we know in part and we prophesy in part, but when completeness comes, what is in part disappears. When I was a child, I talked like a child, I thought like a child, I reasoned like a child. When I became a man, I put the ways of childhood behind me. For now we see only a reflection as in a mirror; then we shall see face to face. Now I know in part; then I shall know fully, even as I am fully known.

And now these three remain: faith, hope and love. But the greatest of these is love. (1 Cor. 13:8–13)

Love is permanent. Love never fails. Those verses don't describe a Hallmark love where everything's simple and sweet. They describe a bold, mature, action-filled love. Everything else will wither away, but this kind of love stays. That's hard love, difficult love, the kind of love that bleeds and suffers for other people.

Sure, we can have knowledge and education, but those things won't save us; they aren't the ultimate solution. Depth is not determined by what we know but by how deeply we love. How many times have we been to a church service where a speaker is unpacking some bit of biblical truth like no one has ever heard it before? Freshly told truth is fine, but it's not the ultimate answer. If we don't have love, then all that fresh truth isn't worth a thing.

> *Depth is not determined by what we know but by how deeply we love.*

The early church in Corinth was filled with highly successful people, but they were doing the right things for the wrong reasons. They were excelling at service but lacking in love. Those good works won't last, Paul said. The Corinthians may have had a lot of knowledge about love, but it wasn't the same as them actually loving others. We need to excel at what matters most. We must be great at love. That's worth repeating; read it slowly: *We must be great at love.*

So, love must guide everything, and love must build people up and not tear people down, and love must last.

When Love Surprises

Back to our story.

Karin and I invited Chelsea and her sister, Sarah, over to dinner. We didn't know yet that Chelsea and Will had already set a date. Chelsea still felt timid about asking us if we thought marriage was a good idea. We had a great dinner, chatted, laughed, and prayed, then Sarah just sort of blurted: "Chelsea and Will are thinking of getting married really soon." Chelsea squirmed. But Karin's face lit up immediately, and she said, "Okay, how can we help?"

Chelsea describes how she felt so much grace right in that moment.

One by one, the pieces of the wedding came together. Many people in the body of Christ donated their time and talents. Chelsea found a dress that fit. Karin arranged for a florist for next to nothing. A photographer volunteered his services. I was set to do the ceremony. We found an inexpensive location that wasn't at the courthouse. The only thing that couldn't be resolved was getting Chelsea's parents down for the wedding. The money simply wasn't in the budget.

Chelsea describes how, on the morning of the wedding day, she felt happy to be marrying Will and grateful a beautiful wedding had come together, yet she was still carrying a lot of shame and sorrow. She felt she didn't deserve flowers or a photographer at her wedding. And she was incredibly sad that her parents couldn't be there. She made a deliberate and specific request of me that when I performed the service, I wouldn't ask the traditional first question: "Who gives this woman to be married to this man?" Chelsea couldn't bear the thought of her dad not being there to answer.

Right before the ceremony started, her dad phoned her. Chelsea and her dad were both really emotional throughout the short conversation. Her mom also got on the phone. She was teary too.

It was time for the ceremony to start. The location was beautiful: a gazebo in a garden setting. Chelsea walked down the aisle by herself. Will stood next to me at the front, grinning from ear to ear. When Chelsea saw Will, she thought, *My sadness simply has to go.*

In spite of Chelsea's request, I started the ceremony the way I always do, with the traditional question: "Who gives this woman to be married to this man?" My voice cracked as I asked the question because I knew exactly what was happening—and I knew a moment of sorrow would be followed by extreme joy.

Chelsea looked at me, crestfallen that I'd asked the question. One moment of sorrow.

Then, quickly, from behind Chelsea came a familiar voice, saying, "Her mother and I do."

Chelsea turned around and blinked—

There stood her parents!

They'd been hiding behind the bushes. I'd gone to the finance guy at our church and said, "Look, this is what we do: We prove that love works. We will never regret spending money this way. We will never regret serving somebody this way." Our finance guy had agreed, and we'd flown Chelsea's parents and two other sisters into town.

Chelsea says about the surprise, "It was just incredible. I could have stood there and cried for hours. I've never felt so comforted and sure of God's redemption. It was like God put his arms around me and said, 'Your sin doesn't define you. Your relationship with me defines you. You never have anything to fear. I love you and will care for you always.'"

But the story doesn't end there.

After the wedding, we hosted a big dinner for everybody. The wedding took place on a Saturday. Chelsea and Will stayed in town for their wedding night, and on Sunday morning they came to church. Will and Chelsea hadn't had much time yet to process all that had taken place. That morning, at the end of the message, I talked about a God who loves people unconditionally. I spoke of Jesus dying on the cross for our sins. Jesus forgives us and restores us. I asked the congregation to bow their heads and close their eyes, and if anyone wanted to trust Christ, I asked them to raise their hand as an indication of a changed heart.

Chelsea's eyes were closed. She noticed a rustle beside her. She opened her eyes. Will's hand was raised high.

That's what I call redefining excellence!

Sure, a lot of chaos had happened before their wedding, a lot of things they hadn't planned on. But Jesus entered the picture and redefined the story of their lives. Excellence isn't about our perfection—it's about the incredible light of Jesus shining into and through our lives. "The Son is the radiance of God's glory and the exact representation of his being, sustaining all things by his powerful word" (Heb. 1:3).

Thanks to Will's decision to follow Jesus, Chelsea and Will were able to start day two of their married life with the foundation of real love in place. Both of them now had a relationship with Jesus, and they could experience a love that receives love from God, returns love to God, then gives God's love away to others. They were experiencing more than love's words. They were experiencing love's *actions*. The restoration was complete.

> *Excellence isn't about our perfection—it's about the incredible light of Jesus shining into and through our lives.*

One month after the wedding, Chelsea gave birth to a beautiful baby boy. They named him Will Jr.

And six months later, Will and Chelsea were both baptized. For Will, it was his first time. For Chelsea, she'd been baptized when she was a girl, but she wanted to express her faith publicly as an adult too. Baby Will Jr. was dedicated the same day his parents were baptized.

Today, more than four years have passed. Another son, Crawford, has been born to the family. Will and Chelsea are more in love than ever. They've experienced highs and lows, as every married couple does, but they both describe how they can confidently cling to God in any trial.

All because love works.

That's good news for you and me—but have you ever noticed how easily people confuse "love" with "rules"? That can cause big problems.

If you'd like to watch Will and Chelsea tell their story, go to ChrisConlee.net.

58

3

The Rocky Balboa Body Blow

Love isn't about rules; it's about relationship.

A mischief-maker.

A mold-breaker. A kid who got in trouble a lot. A kid who broke the rules. A kid who loved sports but little else. That was me in high school. A kid who pushed the line but didn't toe it. Sure, there were some reasons for this. As mentioned, I didn't grow up in a home where my parents followed Jesus. As a family, we were Christians in name and we went to church a few times a year, but that was it.

Things began to change for me as a freshman in high school when I was recruited to play basketball by a private Christian school in the area. I wasn't a follower of Jesus yet, but I was placed in an environment where the love of Christ was truly shown. It was a good thing, too, because it took a while for the love of Christ to do its work in me. All the freshmen at this school needed to take a Bible exam. It was my very first test at the school. I was up against kids whose dads were pastors. Kids who'd grown up attending church three times a week. Kids who'd spent years going to AWANA and Vacation Bible School and Christian summer camps and middle school youth group. They all scored sky high on the exam. 90s. 95s. One kid aced it—a perfect score. Me?

I got a 46.

Coach came around and said, "Chris, you got an F on your Bible exam. How in the world does anyone get an F in Bible?"

I shrugged. "It's all new to me, Coach. This is the first time I've ever opened the book."

Sure, the coach, the teachers, and the school administrators could have labeled me and limited my participation in sports.

But they went the other direction. They knew about some of the brokenness in my family and they cared more about my heart. They were willing to keep me at the school despite my rough edges. The teachers saw potential in me. The coaches cared about me. The administrators had a heart for seeing me succeed.

They loved me to success.

In the end, they *loved* me to success. They saw me through those difficult high school years. It was during those years that my heart softened toward Christ. I began following Jesus when I was fifteen, although not very closely at first. But the roots of a sincere and genuine faith were planted in my heart.

I grew up and went to college and got married and started a family and got a degree in seminary and became a pastor who devoted his life to loving other people. And years later, I was the featured alumnus for the school's fortieth anniversary celebration. I couldn't have done half those things if the school hadn't loved me enough to help me succeed.

When Rules Win

Have you ever found yourself in an environment that's loved you to success?

I can think about any number of environments that go the opposite way. People in these environments might have a lot of head knowledge about love (or maybe not). But all in all, these environments seem much more interested in boxing a person in. Or holding a person back. Or kicking a person out. Or telling a person he or she wasn't welcome in the first place. Or demanding that a person adhere to a code—whatever their specific code is.

Fast-forward a lot of years. The teachers and staff and administrators at my school retired, and new teachers and staff and administrators came into place. In kindergarten, my son, Mark, started going to the same school. Mark's personality type is "extreme extrovert," so over the years he became well known and liked. He was active in sports. Active in academics. Active socially. And he did fine on his Bible exams. But all that changed one day in eighth grade when my son and several of his buddies played a prank on a teammate.

The prank was done in fun. It wasn't bullying. It wasn't picking on a lesser kid. Mark and his friends took some hand sanitizer from a teacher's desk and squirted a blob of it into their teammate's Gatorade bottle. The plan was to wait for their buddy to take a drink. He'd taste it and make a funny face and instantly spit it out, and they'd all have a good laugh. Remember, these types of shenanigans are hilarious in eighth grade. And that's precisely what happened. The kid took a swig of Gatorade, made a face, and spat it out. Everybody had a good laugh. End of joke. He never got sick. Never threw up. No ambulances were called. No catastrophe sirens sounded throughout town. But when the parents of the kid found out, they were not amused.

In fact, the mother was so steamed, she phoned the police and demanded they arrest my son, the ringleader, for "aggravated assault." Sure enough, the police came to the school to investigate. Fortunately, through the wisdom of one of the principals, the situation was defused and the police left. But the mother insisted the school still take drastic action. So, I got a phone call and went up to the school, and it soon became apparent that this prank was going to be more costly than any of us could imagine.

The principal knew he needed to make a decision. Pranks were pranks and rules had been broken, and that called for action to be taken. He didn't know what specific action to take, so he suspended my son for three days to allow school administrators to sort things out. Wow, a three-day suspension for a locker room–type prank. Really? I thought that was fairly radical. But then came the whopper of all decisions. The notice was worded nicely. They were sorry to tell us this. They wanted to prevent greater problems from happening.

Mark was expelled.

I could hardly believe it. Not only would my son's academic life be interrupted, but he'd need to leave the friends he grew up with. And he'd forever have a stigma attached to him. *Hey, you're the kid who got kicked out of school.* This decision was devastating on every level. It was a Rocky Balboa body blow that took our breath away.

Mark felt grief. He was genuinely remorseful for the prank. He'd never meant to hurt anyone. And he fought bitterness in his heart toward the decision of the school. It all seemed so lopsided. So unfair. This was a Christian school, right? A school where grace and mercy and forgiveness and unity were taught and promoted and hopefully lived out, right? He wrestled with the classic equation where rules without relationship lead to rebellion. His temptation was to say, "Well, if that's supposed to be the love of Christ, then I don't want any part of it. See you later."

A couple of weeks went by and nobody was happy. I could see Mark needed to resolve the matter—at least for his own soul. So, I called the principal and asked if we could all talk. I made it clear that even though we disagreed with his decision, we weren't fighting to appeal it. But what I specifically asked him to do was take off his administrator's hat, if just for a moment, and speak to my son as if he were his son. Just speak to my son from one Jesus-follower to another. So forgiveness could happen. So everyone could move forward in love.

During the meeting, the principal was kind, but he kept saying things like, "This was a decision we needed to uphold for the good of the policies and procedures of the school." He was trying. I'll give him that much. But the connection wasn't being made. At one point near the end of the discussion, my son interrupted. With tears in his eyes and a quivering voice he said, "Sir, may I say something? I know you think you're doing the right thing, but you are not doing the right thing. I'm not a bad kid. I know your decision is already made and things won't change for me. But for the sake of other kids, please, never do this to another kid. This decision is only causing people pain."

Love had been broken. Mark didn't feel loved. The principal was choosing to be right instead of choosing to be right relationally. The principal was choosing rules over relationships. Consequences over restoration. He took an extreme, legalistic approach to the matter, and my son felt the brunt of the school's wrath. The social climate of the school was temporarily disappointed, but my son's disappointment wasn't temporary.

The action toward Mark was such a far cry from what I'd experienced in the same school. If the school had treated me the same way they'd treated Mark, then I wouldn't have lasted a week. But twenty-five years ago, they chose to go the other direction. They chose relationships over rules. They chose to prioritize the heart. They chose to love.

The Law, or the Relationship?

In the introduction, I told you the first part of the story of the lame man at the pool of Bethesda, found in John 5:1–7. We talked about how, when the waters stirred in the mysterious pool, the first one into the water was healed. One particular lame man had waited for thirty-eight years, but he never got in first. When Jesus asked the man if he wanted to get healed, the man could only give a hopeless reply. He was alone. Abandoned. There was no way he could get in the water without help.

The rest of the story is that Jesus didn't leave him there. Jesus locked eyes with the man, and the man saw compassion in Jesus' eyes. Compassion is love at work, and Jesus offered to help the man—but the help Jesus offered wasn't the help the man expected. And that's what we haven't talked about yet. Jesus didn't try to get the man into the pool first. Instead, Jesus gave him a specific command: "Get up, take up your bed, and walk" (John 5:8 ESV). Jesus holds all the true power, and the man was healed at Jesus' command. All at once, the man picked up his mat and walked.

The twist was that a "rule" was on the line. The miracle of the healing angered the Jewish leaders, and right away they noticed a technicality. The day this healing took place was a Saturday, so the Jewish leaders shouted over to the man who'd been healed, "It is the Sabbath, and it is not lawful for you to take up your bed" (John 5:10 ESV).

Notice what the Jewish leaders *didn't* say to the man. They didn't say *Congratulations*. They didn't say *Wow, you're walking! You've lain here in your pain and sorrow and hopelessness and disability for thirty-eight years, and now all that's changed for you!* Nope. None of that. They didn't express any happiness at all toward the man. No recognition of the power of God. All they cared about was that a rule had been broken.

Let's call that response what it was: an injustice. And doesn't that injustice cause your heart to beat a bit faster? It does mine. I mean, how can people be so lost inside their religion and rules that they can't see a miracle of God taking place? The religious leaders were so focused on the rules that they bypassed the relationship. They disregarded the joy of a lame man made well again. Instead they paid attention to the day of the week and his sick mat. His sick mat! Seriously? That's what they're going to focus on? The guy just got healed! He just stood up and walked! What did they expect the guy to do? *You've just been healed—now sit down and shut up and wait until the Sabbath is over?*

Here was the problem: The religious leaders didn't understand that the law is fulfilled in one word. What's the word? Galatians 5:14 lays it out plainly, "For the whole law is fulfilled in one word: 'You shall love your neighbor as yourself'" (ESV). Read the verse again if you need to. The fulfillment of the law is *love.* The Galatians passage is quoting the Old Testament (Lev. 19:18), so the Jewish leaders would have memorized this passage too. They would have known the law commanded them to love.

Interestingly, the man had an answer for the Jewish leaders. He didn't try to argue with them. He just pointed them to Jesus and said, "The man who made me well said to me, 'Pick up your mat and walk'" (John 5:11). In other words, *Hey, you can go talk to Jesus about your rules. Sorry, but a technicality hasn't helped me for thirty-eight years. Jesus did. I'm going to go his direction now.*

Compromise, No. Love, Yes.

We are not called to disobey the law, yet our obedience to the law should never cause us to prioritize the law over love. Our law is to love, and the law and love are not in conflict with each other. In the Ten Commandments, the first four laws are to love God. The next six commandments are to love people. Jesus said in the Great Commandment to love God and love people. Jesus said in the New Commandment to love people as God loves us. Jesus said in the Golden

Rule to treat others as you want to be treated. Jesus said in the Great Commission to love people enough to help them become full-fledged followers of God.

It can be hard to keep this in mind. I get that. We tend to gravitate toward rules, even if we know the truth about love in our heads. Truth must find its way into our hearts and be reawakened in every culture and generation. God gave us Jesus to be the picture that love works. Jesus is the incarnation of the Word of God, and Jesus proves that love can do what it was designed to do. When Jesus makes us a fellow son or daughter of God, then we become the expression of Jesus, living and serving in love.

Here's the problem: we might insist differently, but most of us secretly love rules in our hearts. We see this rule-loving all the time in our culture today, particularly coming from Christians. We Christians are quick to engage our culture with arguments and intellect. We love to insist upon morality in the public marketplace. We'll die in the public square insisting that we're "right." But on closer examination, all we're doing is pointing to rules, not love, and what we should be doing as Christians is insisting on being right *relationally.*

For love to work, we can't just preach at people to blindly follow rules. Even God's rules. We must prioritize relationships over rules in our own hearts first, and then live out this love for others to see. The commandments of God are relational commandments. They're meant to be lived out in heart and flesh and bone and blood.

Let's face it: No one is ever argued into the Kingdom of God. No one is ever legislated into the Kingdom of God. No one is ever voted into the Kingdom of God. Our minds remain closed to the truth until we experience the love of Christ in our hearts. The compassion of Christ being lived out in our lives is the ultimate apologetic. There is no defense against compassion. In our compassion, we don't compromise God's truth. But we love others regardless. A person's past doesn't matter. Choices made don't matter. Consequences received due to those choices don't matter. When it comes to following Jesus, it is our God-given commandment to love. Rules yell. Rules shout. Rules hold signs and placards and insist on being right. But love is patient. Love is kind. Love holds no grudges. Love does not insist on having its own way. We will not yell at the darkness for being dark. We will shine the Light into the darkness, and introduce people to seeing the Light of Jesus' love.

> *The compassion of Christ being lived out in our lives is the ultimate apologetic. There is no defense against compassion.*

So, with the overall principle of love working in mind, let's go more in depth. How can we prioritize relationships over rules? Consider three ways.

1. We act our way into a new way of feeling.

Our call is to love others. But maybe we don't feel like loving others. What do we do?

We don't become people who love others because other people feel love-worthy to us. Hey, I live in the same world you live in. You're saying, "Sure, I'd love others, but have you ever seen my neighbor? His dog leaves his business all over my lawn. He plays his music too loud in the middle of the night. How can I possibly love him?" Undoubtedly, there's someone in your life who's hard to love. The person on social media who votes differently than you do. Your slob of a housemate. The crazy driver who cuts you off on the freeway.

The rule-follower insists that rules are broken. But the follower of Jesus insists that love works. And the love that Jesus calls us to is not a love dependent on feelings. It is a love of choice, a love not born of conditionality. "We love because he first loved us," says the apostle John in 1 John 4:19. The word for "love" used twice in that verse is the Greek word *agapao*. It's the type of love that decides to love. It's not dependent on feelings. The point is that we love because Jesus commands us to love, and his commandments are not burdensome. Since we choose to follow Jesus, we choose to love.

If we are waiting for loving feelings to arrive before we love, then we will often need to wait a very long time. How many times do we feel like forgiving before we forgive? The emotion we typically feel is anger. Or resentment. Or disappointment. If we wait for feelings to arrive before we act, then we will never forgive. So we must act first. We forgive first, and then feelings follow. Once we forgive, we can see the positive results of that forgiveness. A relationship is reconciled and restored. A broken relationship is made whole.

I do a lot of marriage counseling at our church, and countless times over the years, husbands and wives have said to me, "I'm just not 'in love' with the person I married anymore."

Okay, so reverse the pattern. The reason you're not feeling in love with each other is because you've stopped creating the environment that fosters the feelings of being in love. Invert the pattern and do the things you did at the beginning of your relationship. Romance will return. Don't depend on feelings first. Act first. Write love notes. Take your spouse out for dinner. Buy your spouse a specific present customized to his or her interests and preferences. Praise your spouse with your words. Give your spouse a big kiss on the lips.

We see this inverted pattern in Scripture many times. In Judges 6, for instance, Gideon was hailed by God as a "mighty warrior." But Gideon did not feel like a mighty warrior at this point in his life. He was hiding in a winepress, threshing his wheat in secret, scared to death because of the enemies of the land of Israel.

In order to fully believe what God said, Gideon had to act on what God said. So Gideon began to go God's direction, and once Gideon began to act like a strong warrior, then Gideon became the strong warrior God already knew him to be. Gideon acted on faith. He began to do the things God told him to do. He acted a little bit brave. He acted a little bit strong. And soon enough, he became a mighty warrior.

For love to work, we must act our way into a new way of feeling.

2. We replace selfish love with selfless love.

I'm a little bit older than the selfie generation, but in this online world, everyone is constantly taking pictures. What happens when my teenagers take group pics? They immediately look at the picture and see if it's good enough to post. How do they determine if it's good? They determine if *they* look good enough. *How's my hair? How's my smile? Are my eyes open or closed?*

It's easy to think of "me" first. All our lives, we're told to look out for number one—and if we're not looking out for ourselves, then who else is going to do that, right?

See, our problem with the Great Commandment is that we embrace only one-third of it. Jesus instructed us to "Love the Lord your God with all your heart and with all your soul and with all your mind. This is the great and first commandment. And a second is like it: You shall love your neighbor as yourself" (Matt. 22:37–39 ESV). The only part we embrace is "love . . . yourself."

This is substituting the Great Commandment with the "Me Commandment." Do you know the Me Commandment? It's this: *love yourself first.* Whenever I follow the Me Commandment, I love myself with all my heart and soul and mind. I put my desires first. I put my preferences, my position, my prestige, my power, and my pleasure first. And that never works. It's a rules-oriented love. It follows the rule to take care of number one.

What's the solution? It's not that we *hate* ourselves. No. The devil's most successful lies are seldom outrageous lies. His lies are very close to the truth, just one or two degrees off of true north. We are to love ourselves—that's scriptural—as long as we love ourselves with biblical love, a "1 Corinthians 13" kind of love. Love is patient and love is kind, so we are to be patient with ourselves and we are to be kind to ourselves. That's biblical love, and that's good.

Yet to truly act in accordance with the commands of Jesus, we must break the world's rule of loving ourselves first and establish the priority of loving God and others first. We replace selfish love with selfless love, the love that God gives us for others. We replace self-serving love with a love that serves others.

How? One of the best ways is to grasp how short life is. We've got an important job to do, and there isn't time enough to miss this. We need to love God and others starting today—right here, right now. We don't have time for loving ourselves first.

As a pastor, I'm regularly given the privilege of having a front-row seat to people's most significant moments. A few years back, I was asked to come to a hospital room where a middle-aged woman was dying of cancer. This woman knew Jesus, and we talked about the importance of Christ in her life. Then I asked her if she had any hesitations about dying. She said, yes, one. She and a sister were estranged from each other. Years ago, a misunderstanding had taken place and there had been no forgiveness. I said, "What about today, right now?"

So the woman called her sister, and right in that moment, the two sisters forgave one another. Everyone in the hospital room was in tears, and we all felt the weight of the glory and goodness of forgiveness and love. A deathbed is no time to hold a grudge.

Since that occasion, I've made it a best practice to encourage people to capture those "last minute" moments, whether it's truly their last minute or not. I'll ask people to pick up the phone and call the people they love and have the serious conversations that need to be had. Living in love isn't only about asking for forgiveness, either. I'll ask people to record videos of themselves telling the people they love how proud they are of them, how much they believe in them, and what they pray for and desire to see in their future.

Write that letter.

Send that email.

Invite that person out for coffee.

Say the words that need to be said.

Love isn't about rules. It's about relationships. Our time on earth is too short to hold grudges or to argue about who's right and wrong or to withhold encouragement or affirmation from a person we love. Why wait for a deathbed moment? Life is too short. Love right now, love today.

So, we act our way into a new way of feeling. We replace selfish love with selfless love.

3. We make God our one and only love.

If we really want to put relationships over rules, then we must make God our one and only love. Once God is put in that position, then we will have the God-given power to love other people. God is prioritized first. Period. The very first commandment of the Ten Commandments is to have no other gods before God (Exod. 20:1–3).

Really, our priorities are a question of idol worship. We must stop worshiping other gods and we must make God our one and only love. Is this a new idea to you? In our North American context, we often think of "idols" as the little figurines that people in other cultures set on their mantels and bow down to and offer incense to. We don't do that in our own living rooms, so we erroneously conclude we don't worship idols. But the broader definition of "idol" is anything we place ahead of God. An idol is whatever we serve first, whatever we give our allegiance to. For instance, money can be a terrible idol in many people's lives. Money can control people. Money becomes the boss. People can worship money. People can look to money as their savior.

So, we must knock those idols off our mantels. If we are truly doing what the Great Commandment tells us to do, then we will be loving God with all our heart, soul, and mind. When God is on his rightful throne in our lives, then any other idols get toppled. God is a jealous God in the sense that he demands—and deserves—our exclusive worship. Love works when we put God first.

Practically, how do we topple our idols? We set ourselves apart, we choose to be radically different. What's so different? God is first, and second is nowhere near first. Joshua 3:5 says, "Consecrate yourselves, for tomorrow the LORD will do wonders among you" (ESV). The word *consecrate* means to set ourselves apart from idols, apart from everything that competes for first place. When we consecrate ourselves, God does his wonders in us, among us, and through us. If we do not consecrate ourselves, Jesus still extends grace to us. Yet we miss out. No consecration? Then we won't see wonders.

First, we set ourselves apart; second, we renew our minds. We renew our minds by establishing a consistent "priority time" of meeting with the Lord every day to read his Word and pray. Some people call this a "quiet time," but I've never liked that term. Why call it a quiet time when God isn't quiet? He speaks loud and clear through his Word and prayer. A *priority time* is a time of importance. A priority time is a daily, unhurried, inspired time to read the Word of God so we can know the God of the

Word. This daily time of spiritual renewal becomes the one priority that determines all other priorities. It's my first priority for my first love.

When we have this priority time, we replace impure addictions with pure addictions and ultimately become compulsively devoted followers of God. With a renewed mind we can love God, love other people, and make disciples of Jesus. Whether we are returning to God, starting a new relationship with him, or continuing to walk with him, a priority time becomes the foundation of our growth as people of God.

When Love Works

We've seen in this chapter how rules are not the enemy, but also how rules are not what's truly important. For love to do what it is designed to do, we must prioritize relationships over rules. The person is what matters. Compassion matters. Loving God first matters.

But it can be difficult to truly love God first. We struggle with our own self-made rules and we also struggle with the "rules" that the world imposes on us. Have you ever thought about it from that angle too?

For instance, one of the rules the world tells us about love is that you have sex before you get married. At least, that's the big rule today. This rule wasn't always this way. Years ago, things were flipped. But today, every movie we see, every TV show out there, and every song on the radio tells us that the equation for true love equals sleeping with a person first to see if you like the person, then developing a commitment second.

Friends, let me just say that when that "rule" is followed, love gets broken. I know this firsthand. As mentioned, I became a Christian when I was fifteen, but it wasn't until several years later that I truly learned to place God first in my life. When I was a freshman in college, I started to date a girl named Karin, a senior in high school. I liked her back then, but I didn't love her, and I think she felt the same about me. Karin wasn't a follower of Jesus when we first started dating. She had some spiritual inclinations, but she and I were both, in many ways, still following the rules of the world.

For Christmas that year, while we were both still teenagers, Karin decided to give me a gift. She rented a room at a hotel and gave me the gift of herself. For the next one and a half years of our dating relationship, we built our relationship upon the instability of sex. We were following the rule of the world. And love wasn't working for us.

After Karin graduated from high school, she went away to college, and at college she became a Christian. That summer, she came home. I had a golf tournament the first weekend she was back, so she came with me to the golf tournament. We hadn't seen each other for a while, so we had sex all weekend long, and I won the golf tournament. I was living the dream!

But on the drive home from the tournament, we stopped at a restaurant. I'll never forget it. Years later, she and I have compared notes, and neither of us had premeditated our conversation. The words just jumped out of us. We both believe today the Holy Spirit was at work in our lives, even though we were both baby Christians.

Karin asked, "Chris, how do you deal with this in your walk with God?" She meant having sex outside of marriage.

And I responded, point blank: "I don't deal with this. I'm in complete denial. We need to repent, because if we don't repent, then that's the same thing as me asking you to put *me* first in your life over God."

So we did. We confessed our sins before God and made a deliberate choice to place the Lord first, to have no other idols, and to abide by the relational parameters God establishes for people. Because that's always what's best for us. First Thessalonians 4:3–4 says, "For this is the will of God, your sanctification: that you abstain from sexual immorality; that each one of you know how to control his own body in holiness and honor" (ESV). We chose to honor God and take him at his Word.

For the next two and a half years, Karin and I continued to date but lived in sexual purity. We didn't sleep with each other. It was the most loving thing for us to do. The decision wasn't always easy, but we chose to love each other selflessly, to grow in genuine love for each other, and to present each other as holy and blameless before the Lord. We were married at the end of those two and a half years. We'd established the foundation for how love works in our relationship: to follow Jesus first and to follow him wholeheartedly. I can also tell you that when we stood before God and uttered our marriage vows, God had long since forgiven us. Thanks to the work of Jesus on the cross, we were both pure before God, forgiven in his sight, and made clean because of Jesus.

The act of repentance was an act of love working. It wasn't an act of rule following. It was an act of loving relationally. When we repented, love was doing what it was designed to do. Karin and I weren't using each other anymore. We were honoring one another, seeing each other through the eyes of Christ. We were loving God first, and with his power we were prioritizing relationships over rules.

That's what following Jesus is about. Love does what it was designed to do when we prioritize God first and prioritize relationships ahead of rules.

If you'd like to watch Mark tell his story, go to ChrisConlee.net.

4

Hello, I'm Chris,
and I'm an Idol Worshiper

Love works when we agree with God.

My friend Chuck made his first million by the time he was twenty-four years old.

But a million wasn't enough. So he kept pushing hard at his job selling financial securities, ever climbing the ladder of financial achievement, and soon enough he was a very rich man.

I mean, *filthy* rich.

In about ten years' time, the guy was literally worth *tens of millions* of dollars. He could buy absolutely anything he wanted. His own private jet? Yep, he owned one of those. Fancy house? Yep, he owned several huge houses, each worth millions of dollars. Fancy clothes? Yep, closets full of them. Fancy cars? Yep, garages full of them. Chuck had it all. On the outside, he embodied the very definition of someone living the American dream. He made tons of money, he did whatever he wanted, and he was even a "good Christian"—a churchgoer, an upstanding family man in the community with a wife and three children. In many people's estimations, he was a huge success.

But inside, Chuck was absolutely miserable.

Pain permeated Chuck's life. Unseen pain. A lot of it stemmed from how he was raised. Chuck grew up with an alcoholic and abusive father. Chaos reigned in his family of origin, and Chuck grew up not trusting anyone. Success was defined by what he produced, not by closeness of relationships. Love was most definitely broken in his home.

He was kicked out of high school and landed in a private Christian school where he was introduced to Jesus. He ended up walking the aisle at a Billy Graham crusade, and even gave his testimony in front of others a few days later. But the seeds of truth that were sown into his young life soon became choked by the thorns of this world and the anxieties of life's worries, riches, and pleasures (Luke 8:4–15). Chuck says his life as a teenager was mostly focused on "fitting in." Undoubtedly, he understood *intellectually* what it meant to love God and love others, but he didn't understand in a *relational* way. Do you know the difference?

We can understand *in our minds* that Jesus died on the cross for us, that God's call on our lives is to love God and to love others. But the knowledge of the gospel must transcend our brains and find its way to our hearts. When that happens, we put faith into action, and when faith is put into action, love begins to work. If our faith remains in our minds only and is never translated into action, then love won't work. Love breaks.

That's what happened with Chuck. During Chuck's college and early career years, pain still reigned in his life. Chuck began to experiment with drugs, alcohol and cocaine mostly, as a way to quell the hurt. During his early twenties, he and some friends were riding in the back of a pickup, coming back from a party—all of them messed up. As the pickup rounded a corner, one of Chuck's best friends fell out and died. Chuck was shaken to the core and his pain intensified. But instead of turning to the Lord, crying out for help, humbling himself, praying, seeking the face of God, and turning from his sins, Chuck dug deeper into drinking, drugs, and the pursuit of possessions.

Chuck's marriage wasn't working. He'd married young, and there had been a lot of fun in the relationship with his wife at first, but nothing in the way of stability or intimacy or real emotional trust. Sure, Chuck and his wife kept up appearances. They lived in America's Bible Belt and kept going to church. But there was never any real relationship with the Lord. In time, the couple had three children. Chuck focused on his work in the financial world and soon started his own company. Money poured in. The marriage became strained and eventually frazzled. The love in their marriage was broken, but the couple didn't know what to do.

Funny thing about dirty secrets. They're hard to keep. When Chuck's son was fifteen, he found Chuck's hidden stash of cocaine in the house. Chuck begged him not to tell his mother. Father and son were best friends on many levels. Chuck was his coach and mentor. They hunted and fished together. But with Chuck's secret now revealed, the way Chuck handled the secret only taught his son how to lie and hide.

Overall, his house was never an emotionally safe place. As a father and husband, he was highly intense and unpredictable. He never forgot the Lord completely, and occasionally cried out to him, but Chuck always sought a quick fix. There was never any genuine repentance or surrendering of his life to God, and Chuck was unwilling to face his problems head on.

Chuck's daughter became pregnant when she was a teenager. The family made the difficult decision to give the baby up for adoption. Chaos reigned in his house, despite the incredible amount of money that poured in. At one point, Chuck was managing north of a billion dollars. (That's *billion* with a *b*.) But his life was full of everything but love. In his loneliness, it was easy to turn to the companionship of drugs.

Chuck's rock bottom came one Friday afternoon when he was home alone, messed up on drugs, and thinking about killing himself. His wife came to him and said, "Chuck, I love you and won't divorce you, but I'm leaving and taking the kids out of the house with me. I don't want them to see their father kill himself. You need help."

Chuck was crushed. He'd hit the bottom. What would he do next?

Not Drudgery, But . . .

Many of us live stories similar to Chuck's. They're perhaps less extreme, but the template is the same. We continually pursue what we want, thinking it will bring us pleasure and relief from our pain. What we seek so desperately only ends up disappointing us. In the end, we're just like Chuck. A drastic change is needed, but we don't know what to do.

One of the ways love works is when we take an action of the heart that many of us initially don't like to hear about.

It's repentance.

Whoa! What? When we hear the word *repent*, it's easy to picture an angry preacher who points his finger at us and shouts, "Turn or burn!" But that's not how God works. True repentance means we change our mind from how we do things to how God does things. True repentance means we agree with God. And it's not God's harshness that shoves us into repentance either. The Bible says God's *kindness* leads us to repentance (Rom. 2:4). That's a completely different paradigm for us to embrace.

The more we learn about God's heart of love, mercy, and tenderness toward us, the more we are drawn into a real relationship with Jesus. Paul tells us that "God made him who had no sin [Jesus] to be sin for us, so that in him we might become the righteousness of God" (2 Cor. 5:21). He also says: "God demonstrates his own love for us in this: While we were still sinners, Christ died for us" (Rom. 5:8). That means that in our sinful state there is nothing admirable about us, no moment when God says, "Oh, yeah, this guy's a good one." Instead, God looks at us and knows us completely and truly and honestly—and doesn't flinch. We have nothing to hide before God, because he sees the full extent of our mistakes and failures, our shortcomings and misgivings, and says, "Guess what? I love you NO MATTER WHAT."

For love to work, we need to shift our understanding of true repentance. Here's the shift: Repentance isn't our duty.

Repentance isn't drudgery. It's not gritting our teeth and clenching our fists and trying harder to be good.

Repentance is our *delight*.

How can repentance possibly be a delight? Repentance involves confession, doesn't it? Standing before someone and telling this person all the wrong things we've done? Maybe there's punishment involved. Maybe we'll get chewed out. Maybe we'll lose our job, or lose our marriage if we tell secrets to our spouse. Maybe our children will yell at us and make us feel bad.

Sometimes the harm we have caused brings about inescapable consequences—yes. But when it comes to our repenting to God, God isn't in the business of being harsh with us. He's not some cruel taskmaster who whips our backs when we don't make enough bricks. Real repentance occurs when we allow Christ to transform our minds so we desire a better way of living.

> Repentance isn't about me turning from my sin as much as it is about God turning me toward himself.

Real repentance occurs when we look into the eyes of Christ and don't feel shame. We quit hiding because we're no longer afraid of punishment. Repentance isn't about me turning from my sin as much as it is about God turning me toward himself. Once I look into his eyes, I'm irresistibly drawn toward him and simultaneously turned from my sin. The direction of my repentance is essential. I must repent toward God before I repent from sin (Acts 20:21). It's my movement toward God that moves me away from my sin.

Repentance is a gift that takes us from worldly sorrow to godly sorrow. Godly sorrow (repentance) is being sorry *before* we get caught. It's proactive because it's all about restoring the relationship. Worldly sorrow (repentance) says "I'm only sorry if I get caught." It's reactive because it's all about minimizing the consequences. Ultimately, repentance is us responding to God's love with love. It's about our love because all obedience and disobedience issues are love issues. John 14:15 says, "If you love me, you will keep my commandments" (ESV). It's also important for us to redefine our understanding of the commandments by remembering what 1 John 5:3 says: "For this is the love of God, that we keep his commandments. And his commandments are not burdensome" (ESV).

Repentance is a movement of mercy. When I receive mercy, I'm moved once again to respond to his love with love, ultimately a love that expresses itself through obedience. When I receive mercy, God changes my desires, my decisions, and my disciplines.

This desire is intrinsic. God transforms us so we actually want what God wants. Paul teaches this in Romans 12:1–2, one of my favorite passages.

> Therefore, I urge you, brothers and sisters, in view of God's mercy, to offer your bodies as a living sacrifice, holy and pleasing to God—this is your true and proper worship. Do not conform to the pattern of this world, but be transformed by the renewing of your mind. Then you will be able to test and approve what God's will is—his good, pleasing and perfect will.

This means when we offer our lives to God as living sacrifices, as an act of worship, when we seek God first and no longer follow the ways of this world, God transforms our minds. Repentance changes from a duty into a delight. The walls between ourselves and others come down. The barriers of sinful rubble between us and God are cleared away.

And love is free to work.

All about Idols

Let me throw another term at you. Maybe you're familiar with this. Maybe not.

Idol worship.

Any idol worshipers reading this book? Can I see a show of hands? Anyone? Anyone? Hey, this might surprise you, but I am an idol worshiper. Yep, me, Chris Conlee, lover of God and lover of people, and the lead pastor at a Jesus-following church. I am an idol worshiper—regretfully. Not all the time, but some of the time. I worship the idol of being in control. Frankly, I want to control everything all the time. I want to control my time and your time, my priorities and your priorities. I want to control results. If I can control results, then I can control preferences.

I worship the idols of margin, pleasure, entertainment, and luxury. I rarely have these things but I covet them. I want the margin of not living on a tight budget. I want the pleasure of season tickets for my favorite sports teams. I want the entertainment of front-row seats to my favorite concerts, and I want the luxury of tropical vacations in all my favorite sunny destinations. Please don't judge me. We're all in this together. I'm a model of persistence, not perfection.

An idol is anything other than God that we turn to for security, success, or significance. It's whatever we long for and desire to please and fulfill us instead of God. Here's how the apostle John defines idolatry in 1 John 2:15–17. He gives us a strong warning against it:

> Do not love the world or anything in the world. If anyone loves the world, love for the Father is not in them. For everything in the world—the lust of the flesh, the lust of the eyes, and the pride of life—comes not from the Father but from the world. The world and its desires pass away, but whoever does the will of God lives forever.

Based on the apostle John's definition, an idol can be anything we love in the "world." An idol can be:

money or a bank account
drugs or alcohol
sex or porn or overeating or anger or a career or a house or a car
a harmful relationship with another person
our hopes and dreams for the future

We might not be literally bowing down and worshiping these idols, but these idols are still idols. An idol is anything that attracts our hearts more than God, anything we pursue more than God, anything we need more than God, anything that consumes our mind more than God, anything we love more than God.

How do we know if we're practicing idolaters? Jesus, in Matthew 6:19–21, offers a working definition:

> Do not lay up for yourselves treasures on earth, where moth and rust destroy and where thieves break in and steal, but lay up for yourselves treasures in heaven, where neither moth nor rust destroys and where thieves do not break in

and steal. For where your treasure is, there your heart will be also. (ESV)

The key phrase is "where your treasure is, there your heart will be also." We must ask ourselves: *Where is my treasure? Where is my heart? If my treasure and heart are focused on anything other than God, then I'm worshiping an idol.*

It's hard for us to admit that. I understand. See, one problem is we pick the wrong point of comparison. We line ourselves up with the next door neighbor, the lady down the street, or the dude on TV, and we say, "Well, I'm doing pretty good compared to that person." But we must use God's standard as our point of comparison—and God's standard is a relational command.

God says, "You shall have no other gods before me" (Exod. 20:3). And Jesus summarizes all the commandments by telling us to love God and love others (Matt. 22:36–40). We think we're living by these commandments because we intellectually understand them. We glance at them and say, "Oh sure, I love God. I love others. I don't have any idols. I believe in Jesus Christ. I believe the Holy Spirit brings truth to my heart. I'm pretty nice to other people. I go to church. I'm lots better than a murderer or a thief. That means I'm okay, right?"

> *The commandments of God aren't intellectual commands. They're relational commands. God's standard does not rest entirely on what we know—it's about who we love.*

Wrong. The commandments of God aren't intellectual commands. They're relational commands. God's standard does not rest entirely on *what we know*—it's about *who we love.* Are we truly loving God and others? That's the question for us to grapple with.

Do you know why it's so hard for us to turn from our idols? It's because our idols are convenient to love. We like them because they never say no to us. They grant us permission whenever we want permission, and they give us pleasure (at least a form of pleasure) whenever we want. We love our idols because they're manmade idols. We make them ourselves. We fashion them exactly how we like them, we set them up on their thrones, and when we want our gods to serve us, they serve us—now!

To a point.

For instance, if we bow down to our idol of alcohol and get drunk, then our god might serve us in the sense that we forget our problems for an evening. Of course, the next morning our problems are still there. And to compound problems, we have a hangover. Or a DUI ticket and notice to appear in court. Our gods never fully satisfy, and that's one of their real dangers. In the end, our manmade idols always disappoint. They never bring the true and lasting abundant life we so long for. Our gods lie to us!

Honest self-evaluation is needed. What sins do we hold on to? What sins hold on to us? When it comes time to confess our sins to God, of which sins do we say, "I think I can hide this one. I don't want to give this one up yet. I need this idol in my life."

If we are ever going to fully love God and others, then our idols must go. For love to truly work for us, we can't merely know about love intellectually; we must live a life of love relationally. Our idols can't remain in front of us, always beckoning our adoration.

But here's the deal: Idols can't just be removed. We can't simply set our idols aside. We must *replace* our idols with something else. And if we don't replace our idols, then our idols will replace God.

How do we do that? How are our idols replaced?

Welcome to the Exchange

We exchange our idols when we delight ourselves in God (Ps. 37:4).

God doesn't want us to love him because we ought to. God doesn't want us to love him because we're forced to. God doesn't want us to love him because we have no other choice. God wants us to love him because he is love, because he is irresistible, because he is the greatest, most glorious, most majestic, most awesome being in the world. He wants us to be drawn to him. He wants us to be attracted to him. He wants to captivate us, and us to put our attention on him.

Any relationship requires focus and commitment, time and participation, attraction and attention, desire and determination. If you're married, then you know the only way to consistently love your spouse is to continually focus on your spouse, commit to your spouse, spend time with your spouse, and participate in activities with your spouse. Long-term desire for your spouse flows out of your determination to be in that relationship. Long-term attraction for your spouse flows out of your attention to your spouse. If you saw your spouse for only one hour each Sunday morning, how long do you think your love would last? But far too many people believe that one hour in church each Sunday is all it takes to delight yourself in God.

My wife, Karin, and I have been married for more than twenty years, and it's true that I don't always feel like loving Karin, but I always love her (and she would say the same about me). I always choose my wife. Practically, I love her when I listen to her when she talks about her day, when she talks about the kids, when she talks about all the small details of life. I focus my attention on her. Sure, there are times when I don't want to listen, but I maintain the consistent focus because of my overall love and commitment to her. My love relationship with Karin isn't perfect, but she knows she captivates all of my heart, mind, and strength. No other woman captivates my heart, mind, and strength. I don't think about other women the same way I think about Karin. I don't relate to other women the same way I relate to Karin. I don't devote the same amount of strength or energy to other women that I do to Karin.

> *Our love for God doesn't need to be perfect, but it does need to be faithful.*

That's what God wants from us. Our love for God doesn't need to be perfect, but it does need to be faithful. Sure, we're still going to struggle with sin because sin entangles us so easily (Heb. 12:1–2). Yet God wants us to be faithful to him. God doesn't want us to have any other gods except him. God loves us with all his heart and he wants us to respond to his love and love him with all our hearts too.

God invites us to delight in him.

Rebuild Your Relationship with God

Broken relationships must be rebuilt. If love doesn't work in our lives, then the place to start is by rebuilding our love for God.

But maybe you're saying, "Yeah, I know that, Chris. I know I need to love God and others with all of my heart. But I don't know how to do that. I don't even know where to start. If loving wholeheartedly is on a scale of zero to one hundred, then I'm near the bottom. My heart is far from Christ. I call myself a Christian, but I'm casual in my belief and I don't really live a life committed to the Lord. I've allowed my success to make me prideful. I put myself first, my career second, my hobbies third, and my family fourth. I prioritize my pleasure over God's purpose. I seek my kingdom more than God's kingdom. I love money more than mission. I have a tendency to want to manipulate God instead of cooperate with God."

I get that. We're all at different places on that scale. We might be at twenty or we might be at fifty. We might be at eighty-five or we might be at negative ten. All of us fall short of God's perfection (Rom. 3:23), yet the beautiful thing is that every single time we come to God and ask for his forgiveness, he gives it to us based on the work of Jesus Christ on the cross. God always forgives us. God always loves us. And the more we dwell on this forgiveness and love, the more our love for God is rebuilt.

An amazing passage, 2 Chronicles 7:14, shows us four specific relational steps to take when rebuilding our relationship with God. God's talking in this passage, and he says,

If my people, who are called by my name, will humble themselves and pray and seek my face and turn from their wicked ways, then I will hear from heaven, and I will forgive their sin and will heal their land.

Here are the steps we should take when rebuilding our relationship with God.

1. We humble ourselves.

The first step is to humble ourselves. How do we do that? We confess we have idols before God. We confess that God isn't first place in our lives. (Did you know that the number-one idol in our lives is ourselves? Idolatry is simply the process of putting ourselves first. When we're first, God isn't first.)

Humility is straightforward. It's saying, "God, I'm sorry that I actually do love me more than I love you. I'm sorry that I wrestle with being a lover of self, lover of money, and lover of pleasure. I'm sorry I have this tug-of-war going on in my heart. I'm sorry I struggle with wanting success and significance. I'm sorry for turning to substances or harmful behaviors when I want relief instead of turning to you. I'm sorry I struggle with the lust of the flesh and the lust of the eyes and the pride of life. I humble myself and confess to you."

As mentioned earlier, *repentance* is not an ugly word. *Repentance* is a beautiful word. It's beautiful because it's the restoration of a relationship, not just a behavior. It's beautiful because it's about who I'm repenting toward. I'm moving toward Jesus, toward the One who is love. Repentance toward God means I gain; I don't lose. It's beautiful because I'm walking toward the One who died for me and defeated sin for me. Repentance is all about looking into his eyes and seeing forgiveness, acceptance, and love instead of shame.

When I look into his eyes, all fears disappear. I am free to agree with God about my sin because he's just as committed to sanctifying me as he is to saving me. He never quits on me, never gives up on me. As I am walking toward him, he's saying, "I love you." He doesn't love me because I am lovely; he loves me because he is love. In my lowest and worst moment, he looks at me and opens his arms to embrace me and says again and again, *I love you, shhh, don't talk, I love you. I know. I know. Don't worry about it. It's not about your promises to me; it's about my promise to you. I've got it from here; all you had to do was humble yourself and turn toward me. Once you turned toward me I was running toward you.*

That's beautiful. When we repent, we agree with God about our sin. When we confess our sin, God rushes into our hearts to forgive us and cleanse us from all unrighteousness (1 John 1:9). When we confess, God removes the separation and creates closeness.

2. We pray.

How do we rebuild our relationship with God? We go to the Lord in prayer. It's that simple.

The key here is not to rush into the presence of God and say, "Okay, Lord, here's what I need. Here's what I want." Prayer is based on a relationship with an Infinite Being. We remember that we are his people, and he is our God.

Prayer is a dialogue where we talk to God and then listen to God. God speaks to us by his Word and Spirit.

When we pray, we're not simply praying that God would give us something. We pray to come into the presence of the Lord. We seek him much more than we seek what we're praying about. We've been separated from our Father and we don't want to be separated anymore.

Prayer is more than talking; it's being in the safety of God's presence. It's a two-way conversation where each communicator is also comfortable with silence. When you see him, you listen to him and feel his love, and then your prayers change. There are things you wanted to talk about that are no longer necessary. You wanted to have a long conversation and really express or explain yourself but it's not needed. He redirects your desires and suddenly you're focused on what really matters. It's in this moment you sense the leading of the Holy Spirit, and everything changes in your countenance. You've quit begging, wishing, and hoping. You're praying with boldness and confident expectation. Prayer just went from a spiritual exercise to an encounter with God. You want to be restored.

Hebrews 4:16 invites us to "approach God's throne of grace with confidence, so that we may receive mercy and find grace to help us in our time of need." God's invitation is always extended to us. He invites us to pray with confidence.

Confidence doesn't come from the quality of our prayers; confidence comes from the One who is listening on the throne. Did you notice something unique about God's throne? It's more than a throne of power; it's a throne of grace. It's actually the most powerful throne in the world because God leads us by choice, not force. It's the throne of the undeserved kindness of God. It's an irresistible throne. We approach his throne based upon what he's done for us, not what we've done for him. As we approach the throne of the King of kings, the Majestic One, the Great I Am, and the Alpha and Omega, we approach as his son or daughter. We approach as a child of God. The Father always provides mercy and grace for his children in their time of need.

Ephesians 3:12 echoes the truth of our invitation to approach God through Jesus Christ: "In him and through faith in him we may approach God with freedom and confidence." That's reassuring for us. Real relational gold.

3. We seek the face of God.

How do we rebuild our relationship with God? We seek his face. Don't miss this: we seek his face, not his hand. When we seek his hand instead of his face, we reduce God to an idol. As long as we like what we're receiving, we'll keep seeking, but the moment he doesn't give us what we want, then we turn to the next best idol. The relationship becomes all about what he's done for me lately. It's a conditional seeking.

I believe this is the greatest sin of the American church today. We've become consumer Christians. God, forgive us for reducing you to a spiritual version of Santa Claus.

Let's take a test together. First Kings 3:5 says, "At Gibeon the LORD appeared to Solomon in a dream by night, and God said, 'Ask what I shall give you'" (ESV). How's that for an idea—the God of the entire universe invites you to ask him for anything. If God asked you the same question he asked Solomon, what would be your response?

Okay, in this moment, don't spiritualize your answer. Answer the question with your first thought. What was your answer? What were your top three answers? Do your answers sound similar to the "genie in the bottle" answer? Our answers reveal whether we are seeking his face or seeking his hand.

In Exodus 33:18, Moses says to God, "I pray you, show me your glory" (NASB). God puts Moses in the cleft of the rock and passes by him. God proclaims his name to Moses and says, "The LORD, the LORD, the compassionate and gracious God, slow to anger, abounding in love and faithfulness, maintaining love to thousands, and forgiving wickedness, rebellion and sin" (34:6–7). And Moses bows and worships God.

When we seek the face of God, we see God for who he is. We see that he's compassionate, gracious, slow to anger, and abounding in lovingkindness and truth. We can't take our eyes off him. He's glorious. He's majestic. He's mighty in power. He's the great I AM. When we see God for who he is, sin is no longer attractive. The lies of sin pale in comparison to knowing Christ.

4. We turn from our wicked ways.

How do we rebuild our relationship with God? The sequence is clear. We do step three before we do step four. We must seek the face of God and then turn from our wicked ways. If we simply try to turn from our wicked ways without seeking the face of God, then we will continually focus on our sin—and that's a misplaced focus.

Too often we cry out to God saying, "Oh my SIN, my SIN, my horrible SIN, please forgive my SIN, just take away my SIN, I hate my SIN, I'm wallowing in my SIN, never let me do that SIN again." It's good to be distraught over sin, but where is our focus? We must look at God's face first, then turn from our sin. We'll never get rid of sin by focusing on it. It's all about the picture presented to us in Philippians 3:8, "Indeed, I count everything as loss because of the surpassing worth of knowing Christ Jesus my Lord. For his sake I have suffered the loss of all things and count them as rubbish, in order that I may gain Christ" (ESV).

Instead, we're invited to pray, "JESUS, you are good. GOD, you are gracious. FATHER, show me your glory. GOD, you are better than anything I can think of or imagine. LORD JESUS, have mercy on me, a sinner. JESUS, cleanse me and purify me from my sin. HOLY SPIRIT, please fill me up to the full measure with your presence. JESUS, I just want to know more of YOU. YOU, O LORD, are good. YOU, O LORD, are gracious. YOU, O LORD, are faithful. YOU, O LORD, are loving. YOU, O LORD, are kind. YOU, O LORD, are enough. I worship YOU, JESUS, SON OF GOD, FATHER IN HEAVEN, HOLY SPIRIT OF GOD. I turn to YOU." In that way, our minds and hearts are stayed on him.

The exchange is as key as the sequence. When many of us try to repent, it seldom does us any good to try to get rid of our idols and leave it there. That only creates a void. We remove the alcohol, but the pain still remains. We take away the pursuit of possessions, but the chaos in our house still looms large. So we must exchange our idols for something far more powerful. We must exchange our idols to fill the void that getting rid of them creates. That "something" is God. God fills the void. We don't just take away the alcohol.

We focus on God first, and God takes it away. We fill the emptiness with Christ.

Surely, our exchange is progressive. It's not perfect. But it is definite. Deliberate. We choose not to bow down to our idols. Instead, we exchange our idols for Christ. With God's help, we consistently choose Christ. Again and again, we choose Jesus. We seek his face first, and turn away from our sin.

A New Tomorrow

In 2 Chronicles 7:14, God's promise to us is that he hears our prayers, he forgives us our sins, and he heals us. That means the burden of real change lies with God. Our responsibility is to humble ourselves, pray, seek his face, and turn from our wicked ways. God's responsibility is to transform our lives. When we do what God has asked us to do, then we can completely trust that God will do what only he can do. It's a two-way dynamic. Our faith intersects with God's faithfulness.

How has Chuck's story turned out? When we left him, he was at rock bottom, messed up on drugs, and suicidal. What did Chuck do?

Chuck humbled himself, prayed, sought the face of God, and turned from his wicked ways. In a word, he repented. He exchanged the worship of his idols for the worship of God. He learned to not only intellectually know about God and say he was a Christian, but relationally love God and others.

Sure, the road wasn't perfect. But it was progressive. Here's what happened.

When Chuck's wife threatened to leave him, he called a friend from church and asked for help. In prayer with this friend, Chuck described how he agreed with God that his life wasn't working, and for the first time he felt an inkling of what surrender actually looked like.

Chuck went to a treatment center where he began to get help for his chemical addiction. He turned his life and family over to God's care. It was the beginning of his way out. Chuck got clean from drugs, started walking with the Lord, and started learning what it meant to live in trust and real relationship with other people. Love was starting to work in his life. But there were consequences from his previous actions that still needed to be faced. Yes, sometimes that happens, and in Chuck's case, the pain would grow worse before it became better. Specifically, the federal government came with an indictment for tax fraud. Chuck signed a plea bargain for misleading the treasury department and was sentenced to fifteen months in prison.

Just before he went to prison, I met with Chuck, gave him a wide-margin Bible, and encouraged him to trust God in this season of "wilderness." Specifically, I encouraged Chuck to read his Bible from front to back so he could study and learn the attributes of God. I encouraged him to keep a journal of his spiritual progress and to give his journal as a gift to his children when he got out. "Show them your changed heart," I said. "Give them the gift of seeing you walk with God."

In prison, Chuck read his Bible for three to four hours each day. He learned that his heavenly Father was patient, kind, and loving and desired to walk closely with him.

Chuck read and reread Jeremiah 29:11, and the verse became extremely important to him:

> "For I know the plans I have for you," declares the LORD, "plans to prosper you and not to harm you, plans to give you hope and a future."

Chuck started a prayer meeting with one other inmate. In time, thanks to Chuck's leadership, forty-two inmates met regularly for prayer. Chuck eventually saw that a time in the wilderness is not a time of God's *punishment* but rather a time of God's *preparation*. The wilderness is where God refines us, speaks to us, and reveals his purpose, promises, and plan. Our wilderness experiences lead to the Promised Land, our place of abundance in Christ. Our Promised Land is the full rule and reign of Christ in our lives.

When Chuck came out of prison, he was closer to the Lord than ever. His life was not completely sorted out, but a foundation was established, one where love was working. Chuck and his wife began to work on their marriage, learning

Our Promised Land is the full rule and reign of Christ in our lives.

what real love was together. Chuck began to show real love to his children. His son trusted the Lord, and Chuck and his wife had the privilege of baptizing their son at our church. Chuck began to work on his relationship with his daughters, and they began to thrive in a culture of love, trust, stability, and support.

Today, Chuck has been sober for more than thirteen years. He's in his mid-fifties and enjoying a long season of seeing love work in his life. Chuck is actively involved in the recovery ministry at our church, and he and his wife are key leaders in a marriage program we have called "Re|Engage," helping people with "boring, bruised, and broken marriages." It's an intensive, sixteen-week class that regularly sees separated spouses tearing up their divorce papers.

Thanks to love working, Chuck has redefined his life and replaced the pursuit of money with the pursuit of Christ's mission. Chuck knows his worth is not determined by what he produces, but by the depth of his relationships. He's taken his woundedness and gone to the Lord with his pain. In the words of 2 Corinthians 1:4, Chuck has learned that Christ "comforts us in all our troubles, so that we can comfort those in any trouble with the comfort we ourselves receive from God."

Previously, Chuck worked to build his own kingdom. Today, Chuck works to build the kingdom of God. Chuck has relationally discovered how to love God and love others, and he's putting that love into practice, helping friends love God and others.

Love works.

Maybe this feels all well and good to you—but it also feels like a lot of stress and strain for you. You're not sure if you can get things down "right." Don't worry; there's great news ahead. Loving God and others isn't meant to be a pressure; it's meant to be our *pleasure*.

If you'd like to watch Chuck tell his story, go to ChrisConlee.net.

5

The Four-Year Marriage

God loves us first, then we love others.

Drew and Melody and Cupid all crashed into each other. I mean, *Wham-o. Crash. Bang.* They met in July 2001 at a college party and started dating the very next day. Instant boyfriend and girlfriend. A quick two months later, Drew asked Melody's father for his blessing in marriage. Plans were set, but . . . weddings take time, you know. Then in November—*whoops, surprise*—Melody's pregnant. Dad put his foot down, and a wedding date was set immediately for March 2002.

Picture a huge, elaborate wedding straight out of a magazine. Full lineup of bridesmaids and groomsmen. An enormous tiered wedding cake. An impressive feast. The best dance band in town. That's what Drew and Melody enjoyed. On the outside, everything appeared to be clicking into place. They were living the American dream, and in their minds love was working. They certainly "felt" in love. Wasn't that enough?

From the couple's first meeting to their wedding day had taken less than eight months. In August of the same year, 2002, Melody graduated from college on the eleventh and their son was born on the fifteenth. Talk about a whirlwind of change. Less than a year went by, and Drew began work on his master's degree. More change still. That's when cracks started to show.

The couple had few communication skills. When Drew started his master's, Melody didn't even know he'd applied. That's how little they were talking. Then came more change. Melody discovered she was pregnant again. With a toddler in tow, another baby on the way, and a husband absorbed in work and study, Melody felt overwhelmed. She didn't know where to turn for advice. The couple had head knowledge of God and were "Christians" in name, but weren't involved in a church. The only times they ever went were Christmas and Easter.

Another boy was born in May 2004. A year later, Drew graduated with his master's degree. It should have been a joyous occasion, but by then, Drew and Melody were having serious doubts about their future together. They argued. They gave each other the silent treatment. They were both absorbed in their respective lives.

A month later, they got into a random argument over the phone. Drew said, "I'm done. We should get a divorce." Melody knew he was right. They tried going to counseling, but mostly so they could "check off a box" in the list of things they'd tried to save their marriage. In counseling, neither opened up. Neither told the truth. In June 2005 the couple separated, and Melody moved out with the children.

In March 2006, their divorce was finalized. Start to finish—from first saying "I do" at the altar to signing their divorce papers—their marriage lasted exactly four years.

Four years?!

What went wrong?

Sure, there were wounds. Hey—everybody is wounded. Drew's mother and father were both alcoholics and addicted to drugs, and Drew had been raised by his grandmother, who never had much. His father died when he was eighteen, and when Drew was twenty, before he met Melody, he was dating someone else and had a baby out of wedlock.

Melody's parents had divorced when she was five. Her mother never remarried, but her father remarried five times. He was in the military, so Melody moved around a lot, particularly in her younger years.

Ask Drew and Melody and they'll tell you themselves: The bottom line was neither of them knew beans about marriage. They were both unclear about what it meant to be a husband, wife, or family. They'd spent their few married years flying by the seats of their pants, making up their relationship as they went along. In Melody's words, "We were two lost people."

Would their love be broken forever?

A God Who Sings

The good news—for any of us—is a foundation can be established even after a relationship is well under way. Sure, it takes work. Sometimes lots of work. Daters talk about falling in love, and movies constantly gush about the feeling of love, as if that's all that really matters. Once the feeling is gone, then love has gone too—right?

Wrong.

Feelings are part of the equation, as we'll look at a few chapters from now. Yet for love to truly work, it must be proactive, not passive. Love must involve action, not just emotion. We don't become great at love by merely learning facts about love. We become great at love by caring for others; by expressing compassion, mercy, and grace to others; by being patient and kind; by not being easily angered; by not keeping a record of wrongs; and by protecting, trusting, hoping, and persevering (1 Cor. 13). And all that takes work!

In this chapter, I'm going to give you more head knowledge about what makes love work—and I realize that's risky.

*Love works only
when we work.*

It may even sound like I'm contradicting myself, and I get that tension. We all need knowledge about love—but we can't leave it there. We need to apply what we know. We must get out there and work at love—or else everything we know about love is worthless. Love works only when we work.

If all this work sounds like too much work, then *psst*, here's a secret. Lean in closer. We can love others because God loves us. The pressure comes off us when we love other people with a love we first receive, a love from God. First John 4:7 says, "Dear friends, let us love one another, *for love comes from God*" (emphasis added). Verse 19 adds, "We love because he first loved us." Read those verses again if you need to. When we welcome God's love into our lives through Christ, the love of God rushes down and fills us up and flows through us to other people. Our own personal gas tank of love might be running on fumes, but if God supplies the gas, then we'll always have the fuel to love others. That's the secret.

Do you believe it?

Unpacking the Secret

I know it can be harder to live out a truth than to see it on paper, so let's unpack the secret a bit. Let me ask you a straightforward question, and I want you to note the first answer that pops into your mind:

Is God happy with you?

I've asked this question in auditoriums around the country. I'll ask for a show of hands from people who believe God is happy with them. How many hands rise?

Very few.

"Not me," someone will say. "God's disappointed in me. I'm messed up."

"Uh, I don't think so," someone else will say. "God only likes super-spiritual folks. That ain't me."

"Well, maybe God loves me," a third will say. "Uh, let's see. I go to church. I stopped drinking. I gave blood last week to the Red Cross. And, uh, generally I'm a solid citizen. You know. I vote. I don't cheat on my taxes. I'm not a drug addict or a murderer or a prostitute or whatever. So, I guess God's okay with me."

"Yeah," a fourth will say. "God loves me because I do a lot for God. I'm a small group leader. I tithe. I'm always in church. And I read all of Chris Conlee's books. I really make God happy."

Does your answer sound like any of the above?

Listen. My son is eighteen years old and a big dude. He's six foot four and 240 pounds. The other night I woke up at 1:30 a.m. and wandered down to his room to make sure he was in the house. He's a good kid, but he was supposed to be in at 1:00 a.m., and my fatherly suspicion prompted me to wonder if he actually was. (Parents, you know what I'm talking about!) Maybe he was blowing off my curfew. Maybe he was at a party making unwise choices. Can a parent ever predict what his kid will do?

Sure enough, my son was stretched out on his bed, safe and sound and already snoring. The streetlight shone through his bedroom window, and I guess I got sentimental because I just watched him sleep for a while. I hadn't done that for years, and as a parent of a teenager I have all sorts of crazy questions running through my mind. But guess what my main thought was when I watched him?

Love.

I just stared at that big man-child of a kid and thought, *Wow. He's my son, and I love him. And I'll always love him.*

That's when it hit me—this is how God looks at us. God loves us because *he loves us.* Why else? Just because he loves us. Are you sure? Yep, absolutely, positively sure of it. He loves us because he loves us. He doesn't love us because of *who we are* but because of *who he is.* He's our Father. We are his children.

Check out these awesome verses that point to God's unconditional love for us.

- "God demonstrates his own love for us in this: While we were still sinners, Christ died for us." (Rom. 5:8)
- "This is love: not that we loved God, but that he loved us and sent his Son as an atoning sacrifice for our sins." (1 John 4:10)

- "The LORD your God is with you. . . . He will take great delight in you . . . [he] will rejoice over you with singing." (Zeph. 3:17)

Add them up and see how God's love is not based on our goodness or badness—he doesn't define us by our sins. He defines us by his huge ocean of love, even to the point where he takes "great delight" in us. He actually rejoices over us with singing. Can you get a mental picture of that?

I mean, I'm absolutely tone deaf. I'm the world's worst singer. But when my children, Mark and Annika, were babies, I'd pick them up, cradle them in my arms, and sing to them. Hey—I don't sing over anybody else. I sure don't sing over the guys I do Crossfit with. I don't sing over my pizza delivery guy. I don't even sing over my staff—and I love them a lot. But I sing over my babies. I sing over my children. That's what God does with us. God has so much love and tenderness for us that he actually sings over you and me.

The work of loving others goes from being a duty to a delight when we let this love of God flow through us and then pass it on to other people. Love works when we work at love, and we can work at love when we are filled with the love of God.

Let's keep those initial thoughts in mind as we look at the four foundations of love.

1. For our love to work, we must WORSHIP God.

If you're having problems loving your spouse, then you'll want to talk things out first, or maybe go to counseling first, or at least text a friend about it first. But what you should do is worship first. Really? Yes. Because when our vertical priorities are established (our love for God), then our horizontal priorities will follow (our love for others).

Here's how I define worship: it's all of me responding to all of God. It's me glimpsing the full character of God—all his goodness and justice and love and patience and kindness and compassion and superlative traits—and me responding accordingly. Usually, that response starts out simply as me saying, "Wow, God, you are truly amazing." And then living like I believe it.

Worship isn't an appointment, either. We don't whip out our smartphones and schedule in "worship" at 11:00 a.m. Sunday morning and call it quits. Certainly, the experience of corporate worship takes place during a weekend worship service, but worship in its totality is much more encompassing. Worship is a lifestyle. It's the way we live. As followers of Jesus, we worship God day by day, hour by hour, moment by moment; we worship because we are in relationship with God.

The Bible uses several different words to describe worship. Three of the most significant in the New Testament are the Greek words *sebō*, which means to stand in awe of God, *proskyneō*, which means to bow down before God, and *latreuō*, which means to rise up to serve God.* The words reflect our priority, posture, and participation. When we worship God, we see him in his splendor; we stand in awe of him, bow before him, and then rise up to serve him. We worship God in totality like this because he is the Great King (Ps. 95:3).

It's hard for us democracy-minded Westerners to understand what it means to relate to monarchy. About fifteen years ago, I was doing the first year of my PhD and studying

*Colin Brown, gen. ed., *New International Dictionary of New Testament Theology*, vol. 2 (Grand Rapids: Zondervan, 1976), 876, 877.

the history of Christianity in China. I flew overseas and toured Beijing's Forbidden City, the massive palatial complex that contained the households and center of Chinese imperial government for some five hundred years. The city is called "forbidden" because it was originally off-limits to "commoners" like me. People could enter or leave the city only if the emperor said so.

Inside the city's gates are all these amazing courtyards and pavilions and gardens and art galleries and palaces and halls, and in the center of the Forbidden City lies the emperor's throne. Steps lead up to the throne, and whenever the emperor sat on his throne, everybody in his presence needed to touch the floor nine times with their foreheads just to let him know he was boss. That's a picture of a king.

But here's a twist: God is infinitely more powerful and majestic than any emperor of China, yet God, the Great King over all the universe, still invites us to come near. Hebrews 4:16 says, "Let us then approach God's throne of grace with confidence, so that we may receive mercy and find grace to help us in our time of need." Can you imagine that? When we approach God, God motions us forward. We don't need to tremble in fear. He actually tells us to be confident in his presence.

That's the God we worship!

2. For our love to work, we must CONNECT with God's people.

The Greatest Commandment isn't "love God and go to church." It's "love God and love people." We can't love God without loving God's people. We can't have one without the other. First John 4:20 says, "Whoever claims to love God yet hates a brother or sister is a liar. For whoever does not love their brother and sister, whom they have seen, cannot love God, whom they have not seen."

The Ten Commandments point us in the same direction. The first four commandments are all about loving God. The next six are about loving people.

In the New Testament, the phrase "one another" is used fifty-eight times. We are to love one another. Encourage one another. Exhort one another. Be devoted to one another. Honor one another. Live in harmony with one another. Accept one another. Serve one another. Be kind and compassionate to one another. Forgive one another. Offer hospitality to one another. Submit to one another out of reverence for Christ. Confess our sins to one another. We are to spur one another on toward love and good deeds. We are not to slander one another or judge one another or lie to one another. And lots more!

With our Western mindset, we tend to live as individuals. But with a biblical mindset, we live as a corporate being, the body of Christ. "Just as a body, though one, has many parts, but all its many parts form one body, so it is with Christ" (1 Cor. 12:12). Each of us is an important part of this body. Even the spleens. We have different functions and roles and we don't all look the same or do the same thing. But joined together, we make sense. We all need everybody else.

Have you ever noticed how book after book on spiritual disciplines mentions prayer, fasting, meditation, service, confession, and worship, but none mention the spiritual discipline of *friendship*? It's because we don't think of friendship as a spiritual discipline. But it is, based on the commandment of God to love other people. Friendship is one of our most neglected spiritual disciplines. Our faithfulness to God is dependent on our connectedness to others. The more connected we are, the more faithful we are to God's relational directives.

When we are not connected to a church by our friendships, we will soon drift away. We are seldom connected to a church because of our tithing or participation in a worship service or how much we enjoy a sermon. Our friendships with other believers make or break us. Sure, it's important to teach people about the Bible in church, but what often determines whether a person stays grounded in that truth are the friends that person makes.

> *Our faithfulness to God is dependent on our connectedness to others. The more connected we are, the more faithful we are to God's relational directives.*

Business sociologist Jim Rohn wrote how we each become a composite of our five closest friends.* We're products of the people around us. We see this principle lived out in the development of teenagers, but it affects adults too. Peer pressure can occur at any age, and that pressure can either be positive or negative. Our friends can inspire us toward faithfulness or faithlessness, toward help or harm, toward living like Christ or living like the devil.

My son's a senior in high school, and my daughter's a junior, so these days as parents, Karin and I have colleges on our minds. In our family's quest to find the right college, we've gone to a number of open houses and informational

*Jim Rohn, *The Art of Exceptional Living* (New York: Simon & Schuster, 1994).

weekends. It's funny, but we've seen this phenomenon played out several times: Very few university promotors will talk about the actual education students receive. Instead, they focus on the relational and social experiences the students are bound to have if they attend. There are clubs and associations and sports and fraternities and sororities and rallies and all-school traditions and housing opportunities and cool campus hangout spots. The promoters focus on all of these because they've learned if students don't find friends, then they'll have a miserable experience, regardless of how good the academic side of things is.

The same is true for our lives—even though we might be past the university years. When we find godly friends, we put ourselves in the flow of godly activity. We go where the current of our friendships go. If our friends move toward Christ, then so do we.

3. For our love to work, we must SERVE the Lord.

Every August, I watch the NFL Hall of Fame speeches. It's one of my favorite things to do. Strangely, inductee after inductee won't talk about how *great* he is. He'll talk about how *grateful* he is. He'll mention name after name of people who've helped him along the way. At the pinnacle of an inductee's greatness, he'll point to all the people who served him as the vehicle for bringing forth greatness.

That's because love always contains a big element of serving other people. Far too often, we believe that the key to life is getting more stuff. We want a big house or a fancy car or the newest, coolest phone. It's all about get, get, get. But the real key to life isn't about getting more. It's about serving others. Our greatest moments of fulfillment and satisfaction come not when someone has served us, but when we have served someone else.

Even in our spiritual lives, we read about how Christ promises us an abundant life (John 10:10), so we start praying that God will give us things, or elevate us to a higher position, or reward us with some great accomplishment in his name. But then we read paradoxical words in Scripture that describe how the key to abundance actually lies in humbling ourselves and serving others. Jesus said, "Anyone who wants to be first must be the very last, and the servant of all" (Mark 9:35). Paul said, "Serve one another humbly in love" (Gal. 5:13). James said, "Humble yourselves before the Lord, and he will lift you up" (James 4:10).

By advocating humility and service, I'm not saying we all need to roll up our sleeves and scrub toilets in Jesus' name (not that there's anything wrong with that). Whatever our gifts are, we're called to use our specific gifts to their full measure (Rom. 12:6–9). The key to abundance doesn't lie in *neglecting* our gifts. Rather, it's in using our gifts in acts of kindness.

I'm the founder of our church in Memphis, and I've been lead pastor here for more than fifteen years. Certainly, I'm not indispensable, but I do recognize that if I quit tomorrow, a vacancy would be created, one that would take a while to fill given the nuances of the job and the steep learning curves of any pastorate. Here's biblical truth: Your gifts are just as important as mine. What if you stopped using your gifts tomorrow? What vacancy would be created then?

Or think about it this way: What if you aren't using your gifts to your full potential? What important job in the kingdom of God is not getting done? The enemy doesn't want you to serve because he knows once you stop serving, you stop growing. If you stop serving, then you develop a hardness of heart because you have an overexposure to truth and an underresponse to it. You're learning truth but not applying truth. You know answers but that's it.

It's funny how we react when opportunities to serve come our way. Too often, our first inclination is to say no. We're too busy. We're too lazy. We have other things we'd rather do. Very few of us look forward to serving. But ever notice how great you feel after you serve? You feel fulfilled, satisfied, helpful, wanted, needed, respected, and admired. You know you have accomplished something noble and right and good.

Serving solves problems in your personal life, professional life, and spiritual life. Here's an assignment: Name the top three servants in your life. (I actually want you to do this, don't just read it.) Now write down what you respect and like about each of them. It's virtually impossible not to like a servant. If you want to be respected and liked, then serve people.

4. For our love to work, we must GIVE to the Lord.

Our giving to God is proportional to our trusting in God. Giving is ultimately a response of gratitude. Grateful people give. Paul, quoting Jesus, lays it out for us in Acts 20:35, "It is more blessed to give than to receive." Are we going to believe God about this verse?

In 2 Corinthians 9:6–15, Paul lays it out in detail. If we sow sparingly, we'll also reap sparingly. But if we sow generously, then we'll reap generously. God loves it when we give cheerfully, not reluctantly or under compulsion.

How we ultimately feel about giving has a lot to do with whether we choose to give or not. Giving can feel like losing something. But it's not. Giving is actually *investing*. Every time we give to God and God's people, we make an investment in the kingdom and work of God. We rarely feel bad about investing because we're focused on the return. Our return on this investment is seeing glory brought to God and goodness and blessing brought to people we're commanded to love.

Chris and Jennifer were a young couple in our church who both had good jobs. They weren't wealthy. They were just normal, comfortable, working-class folks. We did a capital campaign at our church and geared it around a vision: "Building for the future." The idea wasn't just about buying a property or constructing a building. It was all about helping people. At our church, many people are able to find their way home to Christ, and we wanted to help provide that opportunity for as many as possible.

Chris and Jennifer both prayed about it and decided to give Jennifer's whole salary to the Lord for a set period of two years. Hello? Did you hear that? *Her whole salary for two years.* Who does that? They deliberately decided to love God and love others by *giving*. They were committed to seeing people's lives changed for the better.

They started to fulfill their promise, but then Jennifer had their first child and shortly thereafter became pregnant with their second child, so Chris and Jennifer decided that Jennifer would quit her job and stay home with the children. Now they had a decision to make. They prayed about it some more and asked the Lord for help in honoring their original commitment, even though Jennifer wasn't bringing in income anymore. They trusted God would provide.

Chris and Jennifer stayed faithful and continued to give, not knowing where the money would come from. A short time later, Chris received the biggest bonus he'd ever gotten in his career. God blessed their faithfulness, stewardship, and generosity. They honored their commitment and gave this money to the Lord.

In the years that Chris and Jennifer had given their money, our church saw literally hundreds of people make decisions to follow Jesus. We got to thinking, and we asked Chris and Jennifer to share their story in front of the church as representatives of the body, but behind the scenes we were planning a surprise for them as a way of honoring their sacrifice. We wanted to do for this one couple what we wished we could do for everyone who gives. We wanted to let the fruit of their investment speak for itself.

To Chris and Jennifer's surprise, one by one, person after person came to the stage and spoke directly to them, telling them how the Lord had changed their lives.

One woman spoke about her marriage being restored.

Another woman talked about how her family was brought back together.

A couple told how their lives were mended from addictions.

A man talked about how he was healed in his grief.

A child articulated how he found a home and was baptized.

Person after person shared how their life was changed because of the love of Jesus Christ. Each said, "Because you gave, this is what happened in my life."

Chris and Jennifer's sacrifice put a fingerprint on many lives. Not everyone who was affected talked that day, but what was clear was that this young couple had taken a step of obedience in what God called them to do, and lives were changed.

That's why any of us do what we do. That's why any of us give to the Lord.

We give because love works.

I Do, Again

Remember Drew and Melody from the start of the chapter? God wasn't finished with their story. Slowly but surely, they began to see that they were able to love each other because God loved them first. It didn't all happen in an instant. It happened bit by bit, in the honesty of real time.

After Drew and Melody's divorce, they made sure they always lived close to each other for the sake of their kids. Each parent would have one week on with the kids, then one week off.

Melody found her way back to God first. She went to church for the funeral of a friend. What the pastor said that day made sense to her, so she started going to a Bible study. She needed to buy a Bible because she didn't have one. That's how foreign things were to her. She went to church and didn't know anyone and sat at the back, but a woman said, "C'mon, you sit with me." They became friends.

Melody slowly began to realize how she'd been angry at God and closed off from her husband. Christ began to heal her. She started taking her boys to church. She craved the Word of God and began to read her Bible constantly and pray.

After the divorce, Drew knew he had some things to sort out, so he sought help at a Christian counseling center. Somebody told him about our church, and he resisted the idea at first. But then he came and fell in love with the people, and soon he saw his life change too.

Melody and Drew began to notice a change in each other's lives, a change God was creating. In 2010, they started dating again. This time they were open and honest with each other. This time they worked at love. They went to counseling, and after a few sessions their counselor said, "What was in the past is in the past. You're different people now. You're going to make it."

Drew and Melody knew their time had come. They talked to their children about the idea, then became engaged again. The next year, 2011, they were remarried—with all their family involved. They've been married ever since. Today, Drew and Melody serve as mentors in our marriage ministry. Their children are happier and more secure. Their lives are more stable. All because love works.

Ask Drew and Melody what's changed this time around, and they'll tell you a foundation needed to be established in their lives. They needed to align themselves vertically with a God who loves, then horizontally with people who love. They needed to serve and give. They made the choice to surrender their lives to God—and in the process, they found all they were looking for and more.

Maybe that all sounds like a lot of good logic to you—and logic is certainly part of the equation. But for love to work, it's okay to incorporate something else into the mix, too, besides pure logic.

If you'd like to watch Drew and Melody tell
their story, go to ChrisConlee.net.

6

Have You Completely
Lost Your Mind?!

God uses emotion for the impossible to become
possible.

David and Debbie Alexander made an "illogical" choice.
It was several years ago now.

They'd been married for twenty-eight years, and their two
sons, Josh, nineteen, and Matt, twenty-one, were both in
college. David and Debbie were successful, secure, upper-
middle-class suburbanites anticipating their empty nest
years. Debbie, a leader in the women's ministry program
at their church, looked forward to going back to college
and finishing her degree. David, also a follower of Jesus,
looked forward to traveling more with his wife. Perhaps
live at a little slower pace.

But God was calling David and Debbie to something more.

One Wednesday evening in the fall of 2003, Debbie went to church because she'd heard a boys' choir from Liberia would be singing. (David wanted to be there that evening, but he'd needed to work late.) Debbie felt embarrassed. She didn't even know where Liberia was, and went not knowing what to expect.

But the choir sang, and Debbie's heart was touched. The boys sang with joy and hope, and the songs brought comfort and peace to Debbie's heart. In a word, she was *moved*.

Toward the end of the evening, the choir's sponsor explained the children's plight. For fourteen years, civil war had torn through Liberia, leaving thousands of children orphaned. None of the choir members had biological parents still living. Choir members had toured the States for a year, raising money for their orphanage, and while the boys had been away, their orphanage back in Liberia had been attacked twice. During the first attack, three caregivers had been wounded. One had been killed. During the second attack, all four hundred children needed to run for their lives. Caregivers and children fled through the night. Some children carried smaller children in their arms. They escaped to a warehouse some twenty-five miles away, and the orphans were still there at the time of the concert.

Debbie's heart quaked. All the children in the orphanage were up for adoption. Including the boys in the choir. Some had already found homes but were finishing the tour with the rest of their friends. A few still needed placement. Her first thought was a prayer of thankfulness: *God, you've brought these boys to the right church. Somebody here will adopt them for sure.*

Then she felt it—a distinct tapping on her shoulder. Maybe her physical shoulder. Maybe the shoulder of her heart. The voice of the Lord impressed upon Debbie's spirit these words: *Debbie, this is what* you *need to do.* And the call wasn't to adopt only one child. Two thirteen-year-old boys, unrelated to each other, still hadn't found families.

Debbie called David on her way home. "Hi, Dave, how was your meeting? Hey, I wanted to ask you something. How would you feel about adopting two teenagers from Liberia?"

Dead silence.

Then David's voice came on the line, "Uh, can we talk about this at home?"

What Debbie didn't know was that for several weeks, David had been praying a prayer of surrender. Not just any old surrender. But *complete* surrender. The "I Surrender All" type of surrender.

Have you ever prayed a similar prayer? Have you ever completely, fully, 100 percent surrendered your life to God? Full surrender can be scary, sure. But it can also be tremendously freeing. God loves you so much that you can trust him without holding anything back. God knows you fully. He knows what you can handle and what you can't. (And if you can't handle something, God is always right by your side, inviting you to lean on him.) God is never the author of evil. God is only the author of good. Your story is not the same as anybody else's, and your story won't turn out exactly like anyone else's. You can rest assured, knowing God will lead you in good paths.

Do you believe that?

Love Isn't Always "Logical"

David and Debbie faced no small decision. If they adopted the boys, then their lives would change radically. The boys had been through a civil war. Academically, they were testing at a pre-kindergarten level. David and Debbie decided to meet the boys together and get to know them more.

The following Saturday, they spent the entire day with the two boys. That day only helped cement what they already sensed was the Lord's direction. David and Debbie phoned their two biological sons, both youth ministry majors in college, and asked for their prayers and input. The sons gave their parents full thumbs-up. The next day, Sunday, the Alexanders committed to adopt. A flurry of legal work ensued. Liberia soon granted the adoptions. Within a few months, the boys were home for good. As a new family of six, the Alexanders celebrated Thanksgiving together for the first time.

It felt a bit surreal, the Alexanders admitted, but all was well. The boys were happy and were absolutely thrilled to have a new mom and dad.

But a few weeks later, all wasn't well.

The Alexanders' two new sons became very withdrawn. It was only a few days before Christmas, and both boys were extremely sad.

David sat down with the boys. "Guys, what's on your heart? Talk to me."

One of the boys, also named David, looked at his new dad and said, "I miss my two sisters and my brother."

"You miss *who?*"

Seeboe, the other boy, said, "I have a brother, too, and I miss him terribly."

This was the first news the Alexanders had heard of other siblings. It was true. David had a fifteen-year-old sister named Mercy, an eleven-year-old sister named Teta, and an eight-year-old brother named James—all still at the orphanage. Seeboe had a thirteen-year-old brother named Joe, who wasn't actually his biological sibling but an extremely close friend, a "blood brother," still at the orphanage.

David went to Debbie and said, "Honey, you need to sit down."

"No, I'm fine," Debbie said. "I can handle anything." (Keep in mind she was the children's main caregiver.)

David said, "No, you really need to sit down. Siblings need to be together, and there are four more children we need to pray about adopting."

Debbie raised her hand. "Nope. I don't want to hear it. You've lost your mind!"

But resistance gave way to conversation. The couple prayed. They sought the face of God. Two months went by. The boys never pressured their new parents toward any decisions. David and Debbie both knew the implications of adopting four more children from Liberia were tremendous. The children needed dental and medical care. Grocery bills would be higher. More money would be needed for clothes, shoes, furniture, bedding, transportation, sports equipment, and the endless list of things children need. (Karin and I have just two kids, and I can tell you—kids ain't cheap!)

One day, Debbie phoned the orphanage in Liberia and asked to speak to Mercy, the fifteen-year-old sister. Mercy spoke first: "We love you so much for adopting our brother. We're so happy David has a home. Thank you for taking care of him."

Debbie couldn't believe it. The teenager spoke without any jealousy or manipulation in her voice. She was only happy for her little brother. Debbie began to warm to the idea. Would they? Could they? Was God truly calling them toward an even more radical lifestyle?

That would mean the Alexanders would have eight children total. Eight children! And adopting teenagers can be even trickier. By the time a kid is a teen, you just never know what he or she has gone through.

Had the Alexanders completely lost their minds?!

Mind Plus Heart

Let's hold off the conclusion of that story for a bit—and raise a question surrounding one of the prime factors that fueled the Alexanders' initial decision. That prime factor is emotion, and the question is this: What place do our emotions have when it comes to us living an abundant life?

Emotion?

Yes. Emotion.

See, ultimately, the Alexanders chose to adopt two boys out of "surrender" and "obedience" to God, so we could use those words too. But the reason I like the word *emotion* is because David and Debbie had both felt their hearts stirred as part of God's call on their lives—and the emotion they felt prompted them to action. God used the Alexanders' emotions to help them prove love works.

The Alexanders felt *compassion*. They felt *tenderness*. They felt *sorrow* and *sympathy* for these children. They became *determined* to adopt the boys (and determination is an emotion as much as a cerebral choice). The Alexanders felt the *enthusiasm* and *happiness* and *joyfulness* of a new family. They felt *concerned* when the boys grew sad because they were apart from their siblings. They felt *concern* and *tenderness* and *empathy* all over again at the possibility of adopting four more children.

Emotion takes us further in our spiritual journey than we'd ever go otherwise. Emotion helps move us to do things we wouldn't do otherwise. And emotion is one of the things God uses for the impossible to become possible.

But not everybody likes the idea of God using our emotions. Some people simply aren't emotional people—or if they are emotional, they don't want to be known for their emotions. They are "head" people only. Cerebral people. They make decisions based on logic and sound reasoning. Maybe they're even skeptical toward emotions.

For other people, the whole idea of emotion is tightly intertwined with worship styles, denominations, or classifications of churches. Mention "emotion" and these people feel oriented around one camp but not the other. Descriptions differ, but these camps can be called high church or contemporary, charismatic or traditional, expressive or nonexpressive. The camps don't always merge. There are stereotypes to overcome. I get that.

Other people insist that emotions only come out of an evil heart, so we shouldn't give emotions any weight at all. They point to verses such as Jeremiah 17:9, "The heart is deceitful above all things, and desperately sick; who can understand it?" (ESV). And they insist that our hearts are bad and our feelings are never to be trusted.

But they are forgetting (or have never read) verses such as Jeremiah 24:7, where God says, "I will give them a heart

127

to know me, that I am the LORD." And Ezekiel 36:26, where God says, "I will give you a new heart and put a new spirit in you; I will remove from you your heart of stone and give you a heart of flesh."

Or how about one of my favorite verses, Psalm 119:32: "I will run in the way of your commandments when *you enlarge my heart*" (ESV, emphasis added).

Sure, before we meet Jesus our hearts are inclined toward wickedness. But after we meet Jesus, our hearts are brand new. Born again. Changed. Set free. Jesus said, "Blessed are the *pure in heart,* for they shall see God" (Matt. 5:8 ESV, emphasis added).

Different personalities have different dispositions. For some people, their head is stronger. For others, their heart is stronger. But most people can point to their emotions as being a deciding factor. They might not exercise every day because they don't feel like it. Or they don't go to church every Sunday because they don't feel like going. They go shopping because they feel a wad of cash burning a hole in their pocket. They watch a funny movie because they feel like a good comedy. They eat a big bowl of ice cream because they feel sad or happy. (Let's be real: we always *feel* like eating ice cream.) We make decisions every day based on our feelings. So, let's discover the way God designed our feelings to work for us instead of against us, where love rejoices with the truth.

God uses the divinely given emotion of love to lead us to goodness, blessing, and health, whereas Satan uses the fallen emotion of love to lead us to harm and hurt. Our call is to join with Christ and embrace the power of emotion, not resist it. If we seek and find Christ's healthy guidance for our emotions, then our emotions will actually help us, not hinder us.

See, God is in the business of replacing sinful feelings with sanctified feelings. If we want our lives to work, then God's call to us is to receive his love, return his love back to him, and then give away his love to others. (Yes, that's the whole message of this book—and get used to me repeating this message, friends, because I'm going to keep beating this drum.) A big part of making love work is us tapping into God-given emotion.

> *If we seek and find Christ's healthy guidance for our emotions, then our emotions will actually help us, not hinder us.*

Love carries emotional weight, and all sorts of emotions are wrapped up in love. It's hard for us to truly make love work until we get our arms around the emotions involved in love. We need to see that emotion is not a bad thing. It's a good thing. Emotion is designed by God and given to us as a gift. God designed emotion to help us receive his love, return his love, and give his love away.

When it comes to "love," the church has been far too informational. And not emotional enough. We read about love, talk about love, study about love, and agree conceptually about the need for love. But all that knowledge tends to stay trapped in our brains. The knowledge struggles to find its way to our hearts and souls and guts and feet and hands. The knowledge we have about love seldom prompts us to *move*.

And that needs to change.

The Emotions of Christ

As a minister for two decades, I've had countless brides and grooms stand before me and utter their vows and declare their lasting love for one another. Know what? None of those brides or grooms ever acts or sounds like a robot. I. LOVE. YOU. HONEY. KISS ME BABY. RESISTANCE IS FUTILE. YOU HAVE FIFTEEN SECONDS TO COMPLY.

No way! It's impossible to say wedding vows without emotion. Voices crack and quaver. Vows are filled with feeling, passion, and excitement. People laugh and cry with joy. People smile and beam from ear to ear. I've never seen a bride or groom frown when saying their vows, and you can't look into the eyes of your future spouse and expect that to be an emotionless experience.

Jesus wasn't an unemotional person. He balanced his emotions with the normal everyday occurrences of his life. He didn't lead with his emotions, but he didn't hide them, either.

When Jesus learned that his friend Lazarus had died, he wept (John 11:35). When Jesus saw how moneychangers had made a mockery out of the temple, he grew angry, and even overturned tables and threw out the moneychangers (Matt. 21:12–13). When Jesus was with his disciples and they missed a point he'd made several times already, he asked, "Are you so dull?" (Mark 7:18). We're not exactly sure if Jesus was annoyed or being sarcastic, but there was definitely some sort of emotion going on there.

Jesus went to weddings and funerals, emotion-filled times. Everything didn't turn serious as soon as Jesus walked into the house; little children liked it when Jesus came over. He was undoubtedly down on his knees along with them, acting playful, making funny voices and blessing them, all emotional times. G. Walter Hansen writes,

> The gospel writers paint their portraits of Jesus using a kaleidoscope of brilliant emotional colors. Jesus felt

compassion; he was angry, indignant, and consumed with zeal; he was troubled, greatly distressed, very sorrowful, depressed, deeply moved, and grieved; he sighed; he wept and sobbed; he groaned; he was in agony; he was surprised and amazed; he rejoiced very greatly and was full of joy; he greatly desired, and he loved.*

We must see the truth of this: It's okay to have emotions. God works through our emotions. So, let's never be so afraid of the abuses or risks of emotion that we don't ever get to experience the purity of emotion.

Do you know someone so afraid of being hurt that he or she never risks reciprocating love? Real love seldom originates in a place of total safety. If we want to love others well, then we must take risks.

Do you want close friendships? The Bible says to "Rejoice with those who rejoice, weep with those who weep" (Rom. 12:15 ESV). Those are emotions. If we notice somebody is hurting and believe we are invited in to help heal that hurt, then risk is involved. We need to ask personal questions. We need to stay when times are tough. We're invited to overcome the fear that can come from knowing and being known. If we ignore or stifle our emotions, then we are limiting love in its greatest capacity.

Compassionate Action

Consider the many places in Scripture where emotion is shown to us and we are encouraged to either develop this

*G. Walter Hansen, "The Emotions of Jesus," *Christianity Today*, February 3, 1997, http://www.christianitytoday.com/ct/1997/february3/7t2042.html.

emotion or receive this emotion as a gift from the Holy Spirit.

The fruits of the Spirit, as outlined in Galatians 5:22–23, are basically all emotions. Love is filled with emotion. Joy is an emotion. Peace is an emotion. Patience is an emotion as much as it's an action. Kindness is filled with emotion, as are goodness, faithfulness, gentleness, and self-control.

Take any one of the fruits and examine the emotion closely. We seldom think of patience solely as an emotion, for instance, but think about all the adrenaline that runs through your body when you're *impatient*. Your tone of voice changes. Your facial expressions change. The negative emotions come alive. But when you're patient, your whole body takes a deep breath. You think straighter. You act more wisely. You make better decisions. Patience is all-around good for the body.

Or take self-control. In marriage counseling, we can discuss communication techniques all day long, but if neither the husband nor wife have self-control, then the rest of the counseling is worthless. If you don't have self-control, then you're impatient, rude, arrogant, irritable, and resentful. But if you're self-controlled, then your body and words and attitudes and behavior are held in check. A self-controlled person is filled with good emotion, the emotion that allows proper feelings, actions, words, and attitudes to emerge. A self-controlled person doesn't allow for the abuse of emotions. She doesn't swing her irritability around like a club. He doesn't wield his power like a sword.

Kindness is essentially compassion, and compassion moves us to action. When we see a starving child from a developing country on TV, we do one of two things. We either call the number on the screen or we change the channel. Because it's hard to sit there and do nothing. Compassion is definitely not neutral. What do you personally feel compassion for? The question can't be answered lightly because it gets to the heart of who we pass by and who we help. Who do you ignore who's in need of compassion? Who do you pass by at school every day? At work? In your neighborhood? In your church? In your circle of acquaintances, friends, and family? I don't feel compassion perfectly, and I don't always act positively out of compassion. I confess this right up front. I'm great at driving into my garage after work and shutting the door to my neighbors, shutting out the world.

But, as a general rule, I'll tell you who I *do* feel compassion for. Thanks to Jesus working in my life, I feel compassion for imperfect people, for people dying from their own sin and self-destruction. I feel compassion for people who don't know what God is truly like. They think he's all stodgy and stuffy, only concerned with rules. Or else he's a harsh taskmaster, never satisfied with what we do for him. I feel compassion for people struggling with addictions, for those who are being killed by needles or pipes, bottles or screens, by spending too much, or longing for the wrong things, or lusting for harmful things, or hating those around them. I feel compassion for people who've felt the brunt of racism and all of its ripple effects. I feel compassion for the lonely and the downcast, for the single mom and the burdened father who are working too hard for

> *Our call as Christians is not to be known for what we're against. Our call is to be known for what we're for.*

too little pay. I feel compassion for today's students grappling with the challenges and temptations of this world. I feel compassion for widows and orphans, for the lonely and afflicted, for those who mourn and weep, and for those who long for mercy, justice, restoration, and truth.

See, when we follow Jesus, he calls us to have compassion on those he has compassion toward: people made in his image. In fact, Jesus calls us to become the most compassionate people on earth. Our call as Christians is not to be known for what we're *against*. Our call is to be known for what we're *for*. And if we are for love, then we act out of compassion, because compassion moves us to action. Compassion is love at work. Love works when we work. And when love works, then life works.

Love works when we work. And when love works, then life works.

The problem with far too many of us is that we're only compassionate when it's convenient. We choose comfort over compassion. We think compassion is too costly. But Jesus seldom makes love comfortable and affordable. It's true: love costs us something. Love brought a cross to Christ.

Yet love will always pay us back more than it costs us because the human heart was created for compassion, not for comfort. Compassion moves us beyond convenience, beyond comfort, beyond cost. Compassion allows us to truly live.

Moved by God's Emotion

In chapter 1, I told you a bit about my life—how my older brother died when I was only ten, how I trusted Christ at a youth camp when I was fifteen, how a pastor discovered my brother's Bible the same year, how my brother's life verse (Col. 3:2) became my life verse, and how my mess of a life slowly began to change as God's love started to work in my heart. A big part of my testimony is about how the emotion of love is woven all through my life, and how the passion I began to feel for Christ eventually overtook my life.

Here's more of my story.

I was a passionate guy in high school, but I'll tell you what I felt passion for: golf. And partying.

After I graduated from high school, I went to the University of Memphis, mostly to play golf. I was a Christian in name, but still very much mired in the world. For the first two and a half years of college, pretty much all I did was immerse myself in golf and the typical collegiate lifestyle.

At the start of spring semester my junior year, a spiritual lightbulb turned on very suddenly. I was walking through the athletic dorm one night and a friend said, "Hey, Conlee, they're having an FCA (Fellowship of Christian Athletes) meeting. Let's go." I couldn't politely find a good exit point, so I shrugged and went to the meeting. About ten students were there, and it just so happened that they were electing officers that night. Somehow I walked out of that meeting as the FCA vice president for the University of Memphis.

What had I done?! I walked back to my dorm thinking, *I can't do this.* Then I sprinted across campus to find the FCA director, a big tank of an ex-football player, but he'd already gone home. So, I returned to my dorm room and concluded, *I definitely don't want to be a hypocrite. If I'm going to do this, then I'm going to do the right thing and truly follow Christ.*

My first assignment was to lead a Bible study group through the workbook *Experiencing God* by Henry Blackaby. I went through the book for the first time myself, in order to prepare, and God flipped my world around. Previously, my faith had been a bumper sticker faith only. God was my divine caddy, the one I asked to help me win golf tournaments. I was polite to God and called myself a Christian, but my life was geared around me and my glory, not God's.

During that Bible study, for the first time ever, I saw how my relationship with God should be about God first and me second. God's love for me was better than my love for me. Everything clicked when I saw it was my purpose and privilege to see where God was already at work and simply join him in his work. My passions switched and I became passionate about living for my Savior. Someone said to me, "Man, all you ever do is talk about Jesus now. That's going to wear off soon."

But it didn't.

My passion for Christ stayed strong. And passion for Christ is attractive. I didn't have much to say yet—I prayed a lot, and I talked about Jesus, and I talked about love, and I talked about Jesus loving people. And soon, that little FCA meeting went from ten people to twenty to thirty to forty. The semester ended. I was absolutely on fire for Christ. So much so that my whole world began to change.

At the start of the next school year, I began to wonder if introducing people to Jesus and helping them grow in the faith would become my life's work. Maybe God was calling me to pastoral ministry. I asked two mentors what they thought, and both said the same thing: "If you can do anything else in life and be content, then you're not called to be a pastor." So I thought, *Okay, that's a good test. I'll keep pursuing professional golf, and if I can be content doing that, then God hasn't called me.*

But I wasn't content anymore.

My passion for golf was being replaced with my passion for Christ. I kept playing golf, but it just didn't hold the same allure anymore. Everything changed when Jesus became first in my life. I saw everybody through the bloodstained eyes of Jesus. Nothing else mattered. All my passion and drive and energy that had gone into golf had been transformed into wanting people to know the love of Christ.

With my college graduation looming, I had a job already lined up at a golf company. The owner wanted me to develop corporate outings for him, with the full knowledge that I could simultaneously pursue my PGA tour card. I was set to begin the job on the Monday of Memorial Day weekend. My schedule was basically graduation—*boom*—job.

The last weekend in May, a pastor in a nearby church was headed out of town. He called the FCA offices and asked if they knew of someone who could preach at his church. For some reason, they called me. I'd never preached before. I said yes and preached the only material I was familiar with—Bible passages from *Experiencing God.* I didn't know what I was doing, but Jesus did.

The very next day, I resigned from my job at the golf company. The very next week, I started seminary, training to be a pastor. My life has been involved in pastoral ministry ever since.

What happened to me more than twenty-five years ago? Jesus got ahold of my life. I was saved at fifteen but I was never in church, never had Christian friends or mentors.

Once I got into FCA, and God began to grow me up in the faith, my passion for Jesus arrived and never decreased. Psalm 34:8 says, "Taste and see that the LORD is good." That's what I was feeling. An experiential love, not a love like a mathematical formula. Love for God generated emotion in me. God's love invited me to experience the Lord like a feast.

Psalm 37:4 says, "Delight yourself in the LORD, and he will give you the desires of your heart" (ESV). We tend to skip over the first part of that verse while focusing on the second. We want the desires of our hearts but we ignore the invitation to "delight" in God first. When we focus on ourselves, we get the order wrong. But when we delight in the Lord first, when we allow ourselves to be filled with fervor and emotion because of who Jesus is and what Jesus has done for us, then he changes the desires of our hearts so they're in agreement with his heart. When we delight in Jesus, we are healed from insecurities and fears. We are restored to God's purposes, and that's where we find our peace and passion. When we follow Jesus, our joy is complete (John 15:11).

Home at Last

What about David and Debbie Alexander's big decision?

Absolutely, they adopted those four other children!

David went over to Liberia first and got to spend a week with the children. He called Debbie and said, "Honey, these children are incredible. They're beautiful. You're going to fall in love with them in a minute." Liberia soon granted the adoptions and the children went home with the Alexanders.

Years later, the oldest girl, Mercy, now a schoolteacher in her late twenties, said about the experience, "When [my new dad] told me he was going to be my father, I was so happy. You know how little girls love their dads? I didn't get that opportunity when I was a little girl. I was so overjoyed to be adopted as a teenager. I never dreamed it would happen!"

David and Debbie describe the experience this way: "We said yes to God and submitted to him and went along on the adventure that he wanted us to live out. What God has shown us is the power of love. If God calls you to do something, then he'll make it possible for you to do it. As a result, we have a family that we adore. We love our lives. And it all began with us learning to say yes to God."

No, there wasn't much that was "logical" about David and Debbie's decisions. Nothing practical. Nothing reasonable. But their God-given emotion was strong. They knew they needed to reunite these brothers and sisters.

Love took them past their comforts and conveniences to a place they would have never imagined.

All because love works.

That's great news for us, and there's more comforting news ahead. Love doesn't need to be about perfection.

If you'd like to watch David and Debbie
tell their story, go to ChrisConlee.net.

7

Rescue, Restore . . . Redecorate?

Love works imperfectly, through imperfect
people, and that's just fine.

For years, Amy Howard tried to be perfect.

Perfect, perfect, perfect.

She grew up as a creative girl, always taking music and
dance and art classes. But she thought she needed to do
something responsible with her life, like go to law school.
She loved the creative world but feared it wasn't a viable
way to make a living. So, she put her creative ways behind
her. She met a good man, a pilot, and she believed he'd
love her like she wanted to be loved. They got married
and had two children. Life was turning out for her like
she expected.

Perfect.

Then her husband got cancer. He beat the cancer, which was good. But afterward, since he didn't know if he was going to get sick again, he developed a real "Carpe Diem" attitude, but in all the wrong ways. One day, while taking out the garbage, he said to Amy, "Having all this responsibility just isn't my gig anymore. I don't find satisfaction in it, and I don't know how long I can do this." A short time later, he told the couple's three-year-old he was going to the laundromat and he never came home.

The separation led to a divorce, and Amy felt traumatized. She'd put so much of her energy into creating the perfect life. She had the perfect husband, the perfect family, the perfect home. But now, through no fault of her own, her perfect life wasn't so perfect anymore.

Amy needed to become the breadwinner for her children. She couldn't make herself pursue law—she'd never felt peace there. The creative spirit lived in Amy so strongly that she had to find a way to express it personally and professionally. She went back to school to become a history professor, hoping that she could combine a love of humanities with a practical job. For several years she lived as a single mom, working thirty hours a week to pay the bills and putting in another eighteen hours of studying.

Everybody responds to pain differently: some people run *from* God and some people run *to* God. Fortunately, Amy ran to God. In the midst of her crisis, she found Christ. Jesus rescued her from brokenness and began the process of restoring her life.

The Lord led a man named Gene to Amy. They met at the singles' ministry in their church. On their first date, Amy felt God whispering to her, *This is your husband,* but

Amy didn't tell Gene that. Funny thing, Gene was sensing the same leading from God. Six months later, Amy and Gene were married.

Gene had been through a similar situation with his first marriage, where love was broken for him, and although Gene and Amy both felt like "broken" people, they also felt the Lord was leading them to a place where they could minister out of their brokenness (2 Cor. 1:3–4). God had comforted them in their troubles, so they could turn and be a comfort to other people.

Gene grew up in a "furniture family" and was an engineer by profession. He loved the design and construction aspect of the work. As a couple, they combined Amy's creativity with Gene's background in the furniture business to start their own custom-design furniture line. Slowly, they built a successful company that focused on high-end pieces. Business grew, and eventually they had twenty-three showrooms and shipped 350 pieces of furniture each month. They designed furniture for CEOs and celebrities—even Bill and Hillary Clinton bought a piece.

But when the economy started to drop in 2008 and 2009, their customer base dwindled. People weren't spending money on expensive furniture anymore, and designers started going out of business. Amy and Gene prayed that God would show them what to do.

Amy had spent years developing special blends of her own paints, finishes, and lacquers. Customers had always loved these, so Amy had the idea to patent her paints and eventually bottle and sell them, while teaching customers how to use them. Her father, always practical about business matters, told Amy this was a bad decision. He believed that people would copy what Amy was doing and she'd be out of a job. Amy had always trusted her father's advice, but his response filled her with tension.

Here's where the story takes another twist. By this time, Amy and Gene were going to our church. Unaware of their predicament, I had a strange, powerful, spiritual dream one night about their business (not a regular occurrence in my world . . . this might have been the fifth time in my entire life something like this has happened). The next morning, I had a strong compulsion to text them the Scripture that had been a part of the dream, Exodus 35:30–33, where Moses says,

> See, the LORD has called by name Bezalel the son of Uri, son of Hur, of the tribe of Judah; and he has filled him with the Spirit of God, with skill, with intelligence, with knowledge, and with all craftsmanship, to devise artistic designs, to work in gold and silver and bronze, in cutting stones for setting, and in carving wood, for work in every skilled craft. (ESV)

At first, I didn't know why.

Gene and Amy called me. "Why in the world would you send us this text?" they asked.

"I had a vivid dream last night about you and your business," I said. "I kept dreaming this dream. I'd wake up, think about it, fall back to sleep, and dream it again and again. You guys were giving me a tour of your warehouse where you make the furniture, and the Spirit of God kept telling me to tell you that you need to shut down one business and start a new business. But there's a catch—I feel the Spirit impressing me to tell you that you need more than a 'good idea.' You need a 'God idea.' I've never done this before, but maybe you should actually give me a tour of your building this week, and let's see if that helps me connect any of the dots from my dream."

When we were walking through their shop, Amy stopped to show me how they were doing something new with old furniture. She said, "First, we go find old pieces and rescue them. Second, we restore them. Third, we redecorate them." Almost immediately after she said those three words, *rescue, restore,* and *redecorate,* Gene said, "That's the gospel," and I said, "That's your God idea."

Gene and Amy believed this interaction was from the Lord. They developed their new business plan with an eye to eternal significance. Their tagline became "Rescue, Restore, Redecorate" as a reflection of this greater significance. They patented their paints and finishes, and Amy began to hold workshops, teaching people how to make things beautiful and new again. She understood and respected her audiences. She was masterful at sharing the parallels between the restoration of her life and the restoration of furniture. Everyone loved seeing the old and broken become beautiful and useful.

One afternoon, Amy was home, listening to worship music, and she felt the presence of the Holy Spirit getting her attention. She noticed a commercial for Ace Hardware playing on the muted TV and felt the Lord saying to her, *Go talk to Ace about your paint.*

The next morning, Amy called the corporate headquarters to set up a meeting to see if Ace would stock her paints. Everything looked good with the plan at first, but then an employee with clout in the company wasn't confident about the plan. Amy had complete peace about the situation. Two weeks later she got another call. That employee's issue was no longer an issue. The meeting was back on.

Amy went to a sellers' convention. She was reading *Experiencing God* by Henry Blackaby at the time and believed she heard in prayer, *Find the CEO of Ace and tell him that "this is an answer to his prayer, not yours."* Amy didn't want to do that because it felt like a strange thing to say. She even prayed, "Lord, please don't ask me to do this." But Amy surrendered her plans to God.

On the last day of the convention, Amy was walking down a hallway and spotted the CEO of Ace. (Keep in mind, there were about fourteen thousand people at this convention.) The CEO looked straight at Amy and stopped to talk with her. She explained her paint line and said, "I'm a believer, and I believe God impressed upon me to speak to you about our paint line." He handed her his business card and said, "Give me a call." Then Amy gulped and added, "Uh, one more thing . . . in my priority time this morning, I heard I was supposed to tell you that this is an answer to *your* prayer, not mine."

He chuckled and said, "Amy, did you know I was all set to leave the business world and go into pastoral ministry? I believed it was the right thing to do, but the Lord stopped me and showed me he could use me in the business world."

Ace Hardware ended up ordering five million dollars' worth of Amy and Gene's product. The company invested a significant amount of money on a TV commercial they had Amy star in. That first year, Ace increased their commitment nationally with the hope of building this new brand internationally in over sixty territories. They even began to fly Amy to conventions all around the country.

At each venue, Amy has shared the story of rescue, restore, and redecorate. If her listeners have ears to hear, they can hear more than the story of reclaiming furniture. Amy believes God's favor was on the plan from moment one. "I meet so many people who are struggling and worn out," Amy said. "They feel like their lives are forgotten. They need hope. It's amazing that God can take something as simple as paint and turn it into a tool for his story."

And Amy's dad?

He couldn't be prouder.

The Art of Loving Imperfectly

We're halfway through this book, so let's stop for a moment and do a little gut-check. How are you feeling right now? Maybe you're feeling great. The message that love works resonates with you deeply, and you're well on your way toward living a life of love.

But maybe you're feeling pressured, or you're the type who's overly responsible. You're thinking: *Yeesh, I really need to get my act together when it comes to love. Of course I see it, I want it, I try again and again, but until this point in life, I've failed at it more times than not.*

If that's you, then please don't worry. I fear that some people will read this book and mistakenly fall into the pattern of feeling worse and trying harder, but with limited results.

Nope. That's not what I'm encouraging you to do.

We all make mistakes in how we love others. That's the norm. People don't operate from places of perfection—in fact, just the opposite is true. People are imperfect, myself included. Highpoint Church, where I pastor, even has a tagline about it. We say we are "A Perfect Place for Imperfect People." The church is not perfect in the sense that it's *flawless*. The church is perfect in the sense that it's *ideal*. Our church is an ideal place for imperfect people to receive faith, hope, and love.

Loving others isn't a program we do. It's not a playbook we study and apply. It's not an exam we get graded for. Rather, it's a lifestyle of love and honesty where we partner with God and allow him to shape and mold and remake our lives in love. In the words of Amy Howard, "God rescues us with his love, restores our ability to love, and uses our love to redecorate others with his grace."

In a perfect world, we would always respond to immaturity with maturity because that's how God responds to us. We would always respond to crazy situations with grace and wisdom and a kind answer because that's how God responds to us. We would always treat people with respect, even when they don't treat us with respect, because that's how God responds to us. Certainly, that's our invitation, but that's not how we live. All of us have bad days. We make mistakes in how we communicate. We have knee-jerk responses instead of Christlike responses. We get overextended and worn thin, and in the heat of the moment we lash out with words and actions.

So, if we don't love others perfectly, how do we love others?

1. We love others fervently and hospitably.

I absolutely love 1 Peter 4:8–10. These are extraordinary verses:

Above all, keep fervent in your love for one another, because love covers a multitude of sins. Be hospitable to one another without complaint. As each one has received a special gift, employ it in serving one another as good stewards of the manifold grace of God. (NASB)

We're called to keep fervent in our love for others, but it's hard to keep fervent, isn't it? It's difficult to love imperfect people. Even our kids. Even our spouse. Even our closest friends. It's hard to keep loving one another earnestly.

Yet the key to being fervent is simply to not give up. When it comes to loving others, we often want immediate results. We attempt to build a healthy, reciprocal relationship, but it takes too much time, so we stop reaching out. We pray for a person out of love but we don't see immediate results, so we give up praying for the person. Out of love we talk to a person about Jesus, but they don't trust Christ immediately, so we lose faith and second-guess our decision to talk to them about God.

Galatians 6:9 says, "And let us not grow weary of doing good, for in due season we will reap, if we do not give up" (ESV). Do you know what that means? It means *don't give up*. Staying fervent is hard work. There's a season for plowing the soil, for planting a seed, for praying for rain, for the seed sprouting underneath the soil, for the shoot breaking through the soil and beginning to grow, and finally for harvesting the fruit and seeing the reward. All these stages occur at the right time. God's time.

How many times have we given up just before a harvest season? We stopped communicating just before an understanding was reached. We stopped praying right before a big spiritual breakthrough. We stopped reaching out just before the person responded. May we always stay fervent in our love for one another!

First Peter 4:8–10 indicates the grace of Jesus Christ covers our relationships. Love covers a multitude of sins. That's good news for all of us because we're all capable of creating a lot of trouble. When love covers a multitude of sins, it's like finding a piece of furniture that many would discard. But the truth is the person can be restored and redecorated just like the furniture. Have you ever met people who've become the best sort of antiques? They've been through the battles of life and have the scars to prove it. But they are glorious in their age and wisdom. Some people become bitter from their wounds, but some people become *better* from their wounds. God makes us better because love covers a multitude of sins.

> *Some people become bitter from their wounds, but some people become better from their wounds. God makes us better because love covers a multitude of sins.*

Notice how 1 Peter 4:9 exhorts us to "Be hospitable to one another without complaint" (NASB). Why would that verse be positioned so close to the other verses about loving others fervently? It's because love is initiated through hospitality, the friendly reception and treatment of friends, guests, and even strangers.

Hospitality is a broader concept than we first think. It means more than having people over to our house. Hospitality is a way of living warmly, generously, and kindly. If you have ever seen a piece of Amy Howard's furniture, you know she can design a gorgeous home. But what makes Amy's home truly warm is the fact that, through God rescuing her, she has a deep desire for everyone in her home to know they are welcomed, loved, and accepted. That's hospitality.

Have you ever noticed that when people first go anywhere, they can be a bit nervous? If someone comes to your house for the first time, maybe he's a bit hesitant. Or if someone comes to your church for the first time, maybe she's uncertain or cautious, or even skeptical or cynical or jaded. What does a person need at that point? How will their uncertainty be removed? The answer is this broader type of hospitality. Be a friendly face. A warm handshake. A kind word to set someone at ease. Love is enhanced through fervent hospitality. Let us not become weary of doing good.

> *Love is enhanced through fervent hospitality. Let us not become weary of doing good.*

Notice the verse says to be hospitable *without complaint.* Nothing invalidates or ruins hospitality more than complaining. Name one person you want to be around who is known for complaining. A truly hospitable person is never associated with complaining. How do you feel when someone serves you but complains the whole time? Enough said.

2. We love others faithfully, as good stewards of God's grace.

First Peter 4:10 says, "As each one has received a special gift, employ it in serving one another as good stewards of the manifold grace of God" (NASB).

Each person has received a special gift, a spiritual talent, an ability graciously given from God. We are each to use our gifts in serving one another. Our service doesn't need to be perfect but it does need to be seen as a faithful reflection of the grace of God.

When it comes to serving, how's the attitude of your heart? If you don't feel like serving, then you're not going to serve. Yes, I know you're busy. I'm busy. We're all busy. What can help is to think of service as something you enjoy doing. We all do what we enjoy doing. Don't think about how you feel *before* you serve; think about how you feel *after* you serve. We almost never regret serving on the back end. It makes us feel better about ourselves, better about serving God, and better about making a difference.

You don't need to serve perfectly. You just need to serve faithfully. Don't resign from using your gifts! Typically, in any church only about 20 percent of the people serve. But think of it this way: What if 80 percent of your body was paralyzed? What if only 20 percent of your body was functional? How much would that limit what you are able to do if 80 percent of your body was dead weight? Say your pinky didn't work right. And your right foot didn't work. And your eyes didn't work. Or maybe they work, but you just choose not to use them?

> *Don't think about how you feel before you serve; think about how you feel after you serve.*

The good news is we're not paralyzed as Christians. We're not disabled. We can make the choice to serve as our lifestyle. And when we do that, how many problems are going to be solved? When we do that, how many people are going to be loved?

3. We love others with sanctified lives.

We aren't called to be models of perfection. Many of us, like Amy, learn the hard way that perfection is a mirage. Instead, we are called to be models of progress. Again, remember: we've been rescued by God and restored by God, and we're being redecorated (sanctified) by God. *Sanctification* is a big word that means Jesus is changing our lives, little by little, bit by bit. When we're saved, Jesus gives us new hearts and new minds and new lives. We're born again. We're made new. But some of our old patterns and ways of thinking and living still cling to us. That's what Jesus works to change.

Changed lives are what the great benediction at the end of Hebrews 13 is all about. It's a prayer for sanctification. It's our acknowledgment that we need God to work in our lives. It's us being mindful and grateful that Christ does this work for us. Here's what it says:

> Now may the God of peace, who through the blood of the eternal covenant brought back from the dead our Lord Jesus, that great Shepherd of the sheep, equip you with everything good for doing his will, and may he work in us what is pleasing to him, through Jesus Christ, to whom be glory for ever and ever. Amen. (Heb. 13:20–21)

The key phrase is "may he work in us what is pleasing to him." That's our prayer when it comes to loving others. God knows we will make mistakes in how we interact with people, but our prayer is that the Lord would continually change our hearts and our actions so they align with Christ.

When we love others imperfectly, it's often because our feelings are sinful and not sanctified. We've talked in an earlier chapter about how emotion is okay. To build on that thought a bit more, our call is to let Christ replace our sinful feelings with sanctified feelings. See, God wants to use our emotions for us to love. The enemy wants to use our emotions for us to hate. God wants to use emotion for us to bless others. The enemy wants to use emotion for us to curse others. God wants to use emotion for us to heal others, the enemy wants to use emotion for us to hurt others.

How do we replace negative feelings with sanctified feelings? In Philippians 4:4–6, we find this encouragement:

> Rejoice in the Lord always; again I will say, rejoice. Let your reasonableness be known to everyone. The Lord is at hand; do not be anxious about anything, but in everything by prayer and supplication with thanksgiving let your requests be made known to God. (ESV)

Note the first phrase. Why does Paul use "rejoice" twice? It's because we need more than one reminder to rejoice in the Lord. The muck and mire of the world can be too thick. So, we need a reminder to allow God to sanctify us through and through, to replace our sinful feelings with sanctified feelings.

The second phrase is also key—"let your reasonableness be known to everyone." The word *reasonableness* means gentleness, sensibleness, levelheadedness, unselfishness, mercy, tolerance, and patience. The idea is that in our interactions with other people, we lead with a soft touch, not a harsh shove. We lead with fairness and compassion, not toughness and grouchiness.

And we are to love others without being anxious about anything. That's hard, isn't it? Because there's a lot of pressure in life and many reasons to be anxious. But God's call to us is to replace anxious feelings with prayer and thanksgiving. Instead of churning about things, we are to let our requests be made known to God. Here's an assignment that will radically change your attitude: begin your day by writing down five things you are thankful for.

Absolutely, the enemy attacks our minds and hearts and actions with negativity. We need to guard ourselves from negative thoughts because negative thoughts lead to negative actions. The enemy comes to steal, kill, and destroy, but God gives us peace—and we must choose peace. How do we do that?

The solution is found one verse later, in Philippians 4:8—we focus on whatever is true and noble and right. In prayer we say, "Holy Spirit, please show me what's true versus what's a lie. Help keep my mind on that which is honorable, pure, lovely, commendable, excellent, and praiseworthy."

Can you imagine the force for good you would become if you walked through your circle of influence as someone who focused

Can you imagine the force for good you would become if you walked through your circle of influence as someone who focused on what was true, honorable, just, pure, lovely, commendable, excellent, and worthy of praise?

on what was true, honorable, just, pure, lovely, commendable, excellent, and worthy of praise? Your marriage. Your job. Your school. Your family. Your friends. Your social media connections. Scripture says, "Think about these things." In other words, dwell on these things, practice these things, let these things run through your mind continually.

Imperfection in Relationship

Will we love others imperfectly? Yes. Absolutely we will. We will need to ask forgiveness of others and admit that we make mistakes. Following Jesus is a relational process. When we follow Christ, he forgives us immediately, but the freedom we have in Christ often takes a while to show itself in our lives. Freedom is a progressive work of God, a life of walking two steps forward and one step back, and so on.

The evidence of repentance in our lives is when we fall down but don't stay down. We are not knocked out. We get right back up again. We're still standing. We're still fighting. First Timothy 6:12 says, "Fight the good fight of the faith. Take hold of the eternal life to which you were called and about which you made the good confession in the presence of many witnesses" (ESV).

Amy Howard had every reason to live in defeat. Her Plan A did not work. The perfect life she imagined became a perfect nightmare. Yet what I love about Amy's story is that, through God's strength, she got back up off the mat determined not only to make a way for her family, but to give hope to anyone whose life had been shattered.

This all goes into how we live. We live with huge love, yet we live imperfectly. So, we live lives of big, imperfect love. That's our new mission in life.

If you'd like to watch Amy tell her
story, go to ChrisConlee.net.

8

Too Much Love Doesn't Exist

Our mission is to love.

Twins Demarcus and Jemarcus were born and raised in a Memphis ghetto. They knew poverty firsthand, and right after graduating from high school, they encountered the cruelties of being in the wrong place at the wrong time. They were eighteen years old, and their older brother and another friend picked them up in a car to take them someplace. On the way over to their destination, the older brother said, "Hey, we gotta make a stop first," and pulled into an apartment complex and parked the car. He and the friend ran up to an apartment, kicked in the door, and came out with a TV and a couple of watches.

The twins never went inside the apartment. They weren't in on the plan. They didn't even realize what was happening until the door was kicked in. They were shocked and scared, screaming at the others to get out of there.

But it was too late. A neighbor got the older brother's license plate number and called the police. The four young men were soon arrested. The twins were considered accomplices and sent to jail along with the other two. The twins did some time, then were paroled early for good behavior. They moved in with an uncle and were able to go back to their jobs as part-time janitors. Next to their brother, this uncle was the only relative they had. Their mother was deceased. Their father was in and out of their lives. The twins were just happy to be out of the joint, but in many ways their lives were still chaotic.

They met a man who ran a vitamin supplement business who'd just moved to Memphis. He asked them if they wanted to work for him in a part-time capacity, and the twins said yes. The guy was a believer, looking for a church to attend, and Highpoint was the first church they all came to. The twins had never before seen or heard anything like what they encountered during a Sunday service, and their response was immediately enthusiastic. For several weeks, each time they came, they raised their hands to trust Christ. The friend with the vitamin business was relocated to another city, but the twins stayed at Highpoint. They knew something good was happening in their lives, although at that point they didn't quite know what.

One of our pastors, Josh Maze, sensed the Holy Spirit talking to him, saying, *There's something bigger to this. There's something really good about to happen in these twins' lives.* So, Josh and his wife, Stacie, took the twins out to lunch. The twins had been raised in poverty and had never been to a restaurant where they were able to order what they wanted off the menu. When the waitress came over to take their order, the twins didn't know what to do. Josh says about the experience, "The Lord spoke clearly to Stacie and me at the same time. The word was: 'You can't love them too much.'"

Josh and Stacie were in their late twenties and had no children of their own yet. They reached out to the twins and started developing a friendship with them. They had them over for dinner in their home. If the twins needed rides, they'd take them. These actions weren't handouts. Josh and Stacie were sincere about their friendship. They weren't asking the twins to get their act together or to get cleaned up. They were simply loving the twins exactly where they were. They listened to music together. They played basketball together. They had spiritual discussions, but not all the time.

Months went by, and the relationship gradually morphed from a friendship into more of a mentoring relationship. Even though the twins were out of jail, they still had court dates they needed to make and all sorts of attorney fees to pay. Josh and Stacie didn't give them any sizable amounts of money, but simply walked with them in the world of stewardship and taught them how to organize their schedules and make things happen.

All this time, the twins lived with their uncle at his apartment. One day, the uncle went to go to work and discovered the wheels had been stolen from his car. The twins had nothing to do with it, but the uncle was fed up with the neighborhood—so he moved out and left the twins there with the rent to pay on their own. Their job situations were still iffy; they had almost no money to their names. They couldn't make rent and soon were evicted from the apartment. They had nowhere to go.

They called Josh and Stacie.

Josh and Stacie didn't hesitate. The twins needed to be out of their apartment that same day. Josh and Stacie came over, loaded up the twins' belongings in their Nissan Maxima, and drove them over to their place—a tiny house with only one bathroom. On the way over, the twins cried.

Little by little, more of their story came out. The twins had been through a lot. When they were just little kids, one of their parents beat them, held them under water in the bathtub, and broke an arm. They'd been neglected and left by themselves for days on end. One boy had a scar from digging in a trash can as a three-year-old, looking for food.

Step by step, Josh and Stacie helped the twins piece together their lives. They taught them about love and loyalty and servanthood. They modeled effective communication skills and conflict resolution. They helped them get full-time jobs, driver's licenses, a car, and eventually, their own apartment. The journey wasn't all easy. The twins would come in at three in the morning and make noise when Josh needed to be up by five. They often wouldn't take care of their rooms. Sometimes they used inappropriate language. Arguments were had. For Josh and Stacie, it was a continual exercise in patience, gentleness, goodness, forgiveness, and kindness. They reminded themselves of the word they'd heard from the Lord: *You can't love them too much.*

Many others in the church helped too. The twins were able to buy their car, a used Camry with low miles, because someone in the church sold it to them ridiculously cheap. Another person in the church gave them jobs in his warehouse—and the jobs came with benefits. A family owned a boat and took the twins to the lake a bunch of times. The twins began to serve in the church as hosts in the Student VIP room, where first-time guests go to get connected with other students. They each learned the importance of tithing and began to give back to the Lord. They made great friends in their own age group.

When the twins turned twenty, Josh and Stacie threw them a big surprise birthday party. A bunch of people from the church came over, and everybody brought presents. The twins just stared at their gifts. It was the first birthday party they'd ever had.

The twins are doing great today. They went from being virtually homeless, cast out on the streets, to a place where they're self-sufficient in their jobs and living situations. They're both maturing well in life and in their spiritual walks, and they serve in a variety of ways at church. They have really turned from boys into men—and it's great to see.

As a church, we learned several things about our interaction with the twins. We saw how love is a process and takes time, but also how love really can change people's lives in amazing ways. Love isn't always easy. Josh and Stacie in particular were inconvenienced by love, and love cost them time and mental energy and space in their house and financial outlay. But when love works, life works. The twins' lives began to work when Josh and Stacie loved them well and proved that love works.

We're clear on this point: We didn't rescue the twins. The love of Jesus rescued the twins. Josh and Stacie modeled what it means to be friends with all people. Our call is not to criticize people or put them down but to walk through the process with them of doing life together.

No matter what, our mission is to love.

We Have a Job to Do

When I say "our mission is to love," I'm talking about each and every one of us who follow Jesus. What's surprising is that when we know about this mission, and live by this mission, the benefit flows back to us. When we understand our job is to love and then actually do that—we love other people—surely they reap the reward of that love, but we do too!

Think of it this way. What does the experience of "going to church" look like for you? If you're like many people, you'll sort of wander into church on Sunday morning, maybe shake hands with the greeter on the way in, find your way to your seat, maybe nod to one or two people whose faces look familiar, sing along with some of the songs, listen to the message, nod at a few people on the way out, and then leave. You'll be encouraged and edified in a number of ways, but you'll still feel vaguely hollow—like you caught a lot of good things but still missed out on something important.

What's missing is your mission. It's a general attitude you adopt—and then live out—to love people in the process. See, as followers of Christ we have a job to do—and this job needs to be done both inside and outside the walls of the church. Church is not about attending. It's about loving.

So, use the same scenario, but adopt the mission and see what happens. As you head into church on a Sunday morning, you've got your eyes open to see who's new. Who needs a friendly smile and a warm handshake? It's your job to go up to that person and initiate a greeting and a conversation. Yes, yours. And it's my job too. And it's that person's job to go up to you. But maybe that person doesn't know that yet. Or maybe that person has had a really difficult week. Or maybe that person is brand-new to Jesus and has no idea what it means to live in an extended community where people prove that love works.

The smile and the handshake are only the beginning. After that, as the relationship permits, you initiate conversations where you ask warm and loving, open-ended questions. You are genuinely interested in what the person has to say. You listen more than you speak, and you remember things about the person's life so you can further the conversation and the relationship the next time you meet.

Let's keep going. What is your mission when you go home and see your neighbor across the fence mowing their lawn? What's your mission when you head into the office or school on Monday morning? When you pick up your kid from soccer practice? When you interact with the checkout clerk at the grocery store? When you head to your family reunion and meet a million aunts and uncles and cousins you haven't seen in years? Yes, even when you get pulled over by a police officer for going over the speed limit?

Your mission is to love.

A full-fledged conversation might not be possible in each of those situations, yet the overall theme of loving others remains at the forefront of every interaction. When we understand that we have a purposeful job to do, then so much else in life gets put into perspective.

Paul said, "Whatever happens, conduct yourselves in a manner worthy of the gospel of Christ" (Phil. 1:27). Too often we read this verse and think it's an admonition to be on our best behavior at all times, to toe the line. Is that it? No. When we conduct ourselves in a manner worthy of Christ, we're not talking about *rule-keeping* as we talked about earlier. We're talking about *relationships*.

The glue that makes those relationships work is *love*. When we walk in a manner worthy of Christ, we lead with love, our mission is to love, our job is to love, and our emphasis is to love. We are always asking ourselves: *What's the most loving thing I can do? How can I lead a life of love?*

Let's make this practical. What does it look like to lead a life of love, to be on a mission of love?

1. Living out a mission of love means we strategically engage with people.

Josh and Stacie *noticed* the twins in church. This was the beginning of their friendship. Demarcus and Jemarcus didn't simply wander in and remain nameless to the people around them. Josh and Stacie had their eyes open, looking to see who needed to be loved.

Love doesn't work when we retreat from people, when we shelter ourselves from people, when we act like we need to protect ourselves from people. Jesus wasn't afraid to strategically engage with people. He noticed people: a blind man who needed to see, a Samaritan woman at a well in the noonday sun, a height-challenged man named Zacchaeus who'd climbed a tree. Certainly, it's okay to take short breaks from being with people. Even Jesus did that. He frequently went off by himself to recharge, often spending all night in prayer to the Father. But then Jesus came back and engaged with people again. Sometimes it was with multitudes. Sometimes it was with smaller groups of seventy, twelve, and three. Sometimes just one-on-one.

And Jesus was big on asking people questions. Certainly, he taught others, but just think of all the questions Jesus asked:

- Who of you by worrying can add a single hour to his life?
- Who do people say the Son of Man is?
- Who is the greatest in the kingdom of heaven?
- What good will it be for a man if he gains the whole world yet forfeits his soul?
- Can you drink the cup I'm going to drink?
- What do you want me to do for you?
- Does this offend you?
- Why do you look at a speck of sawdust in your brother's eye and pay no attention to the plank in your own eye?
- Why are you so afraid—do you still have no faith?
- Why do you entertain evil thoughts in your hearts?

. . . and that's only a fraction of the questions Jesus asked. Some brainy mathematician counted it up, and apparently Jesus asked 307 questions as recorded in the Gospels. The point is that Jesus didn't tell people what to do. He didn't argue. He didn't debate. Instead, he engaged people in conversations where he was able to move beyond small talk to get to the core issues of their lives, and he often did so with questions. He was able to see into the souls of people and deal with their issues. That's the mission of love at work.

When we ask questions of people, and then truly listen to them, this becomes a good entry point of love. Listening causes people to receive our friendship because we're paying attention to their story. Listening is the ultimate form of relationship-building. We all love to talk about ourselves, but we also love it when people take interest in us. When somebody listens to you, it makes you feel valued. It means that the person is slowing down his busyness and making you a priority. When a person listens to you, it shows she cares.

It's so key we grasp this point; it will literally change the way we interact with people. Jesus didn't walk around acting like a big shot. He didn't announce who he was. He didn't lead with his résumé. He wasn't in the business of calling attention to himself or making himself the star of the show. When he saw the crowds, he had compassion on them. He looked into the faces and saw individuals. He asked questions of people and reached their hearts.

So, how do you actually ask effective questions? Well, very simply, you practice. Some questions can be answered with a blatant yes or no. Those are typically the questions to avoid. We want to ask open-ended questions where a person needs to think about an answer and then respond with his or her life experience. Start slow. It's okay to break the ice by talking about the weather or sports or whatever happens to be convenient. But don't stop there; ask an open-ended question and see what happens. More often than not, your question will help draw the person out. Be careful of asking too personal of a question before you truly know someone. You're not there to be a psychologist, a courtroom attorney, or a journalist. You're there to be a friend.

One of the best techniques for asking effective questions is to ask a *what* question, then follow that up with a related *why* question. For example:

Person 1: "*What* do you do for a living?"

Person 2: "Oh, I'm an architect."

Person 1: "How interesting. *Why* did you go into that job field?"

Can you see how the *why* question inches under the surface? Suddenly, you've got the makings of a good conversation. You've given the person the opportunity to talk about her motives and values. The person might talk about his history; why he made the choices he did in years past. Maybe the person will talk about her regrets (*Well, I always wanted to be an actor, but I thought architecture was more practical*). Maybe the person will talk about his hopes and ambitions. You are not talking about merely sports or the weather anymore. You have opened up a whole new realm of your friendship by noticing people, asking questions, and listening.

2. Living out a mission of love means we aren't afraid of messy lives.

Compassion moves us past comfort, convenience, and cost. Jesus wasn't afraid of engaging with people whose lives were anything but "put together." He engaged with sick and broken people. He engaged with complicated people. He engaged with angry people and people in spiritually dark places.

By contrast, the Pharisees and teachers of the law avoided messy people. In Luke 7:36–50, a woman with a sinful past anointed the feet of Jesus with perfume when he was teaching in a Pharisee's house. The Pharisees grumbled at the lavish display, but the passage is a beautiful picture of Jesus receiving love, giving love, and even affirming the "sinner" in the presence of the "religious."

Jesus didn't love people by escaping from them. He didn't walk around with an attitude that said, *I'm going to protect myself from all these messy people.* No, he taught his disciples to be "salt" and "light" (Matt. 5:13–16), to be in the world but not of the world. What does it mean to be salt and light?

Salt is a preserving agent. It keeps food from going rotten. Salt is a flavoring. It adds spice and variety to anything bland. Salt also creates thirst, the way we can help create in people a thirst for Christ.

Light allows people to see in the dark. Light illuminates and makes things visible. A shining light can show people the way. A light can prevent people from stumbling around and hurting themselves. A light is a beacon. A lighthouse directs people to a safe harbor. Light is an agency of hope that helps bring people home again.

One of my favorite titles of Christ is that he was called a "friend of sinners" (Luke 7:34). The title was hurled at Christ by his enemies, and some well-meaning theologians throughout the years have scorned the title, worrying that it implies a chumminess with sin. That's probably how Christ's enemies used the term—as an insult, a warning. *Watch out for that Jesus—he pals around with evil.*

Yet the beauty of this title is that it shows Christ's love for people, no matter their condition. He felt perfectly comfortable associating with the outcast and marginalized of his day, the people who weren't considered religious. Jesus was the embodiment of all goodness and righteousness and holiness and purity, yet he didn't distance himself from those who needed him most. Romans 2:4 reminds us that God's *kindness* leads people to repentance. It isn't condemnation that leads people to repentance. It's kindness.

Often the fear with being a friend of sinners is that we'll somehow be corrupted in the process, or we'll embrace the sin along with the friendship—and we'll talk about this tension more in a chapter to come. For now, consider how throughout history the church has largely reacted to cultural movements with suspicion, fear, and separation. The cultural upheaval in the 1960s and the social revolutions that championed "sex, drugs, and rock 'n' roll" are prime examples. Thoughtful Christians withdrew from certain industries because they were labeled by the church as "impure industries," and so by removing ourselves, we inadvertently accelerated the corruption. Music. Dance. Art. Literature. Universities. Journalism. Television. Movies. These industries decayed faster because we removed the light from the darkness. As Christians, we can be so afraid of compromise that we forget our compassion.

Jesus never calls us to escape the culture. Yet at the same time, Jesus never embraced the culture—not in the sense that he embraced sin. Rather, Jesus engaged the culture, and the way he did this was to become a friend of sinners. He never compromised who he was and he never compromised the truth, yet he always led with love. The glorious result was that the people who were furthest from God longed to be near him.

Paul, in 1 Corinthians 9:19–22, talks about how he was free in Christ, yet took that freedom and made himself a slave to everyone in order to win as many people as possible. To the Jews, he became a Jew to win the Jews. To those not having the law, he became like one not having the law so as to win those not having the law. He closes by saying, "I have become all things to all people so that by all possible means I might save some" (v. 22). What was Paul's goal in life? It was a mission of love to win others to Christ. Paul used his freedom to serve, to reach others, to introduce people to Jesus.

Certainly, we need discernment. If you're a former alcoholic who's still tempted by drinking, then I wouldn't counsel you to have a ministry in bars. But we Christians too often long for black-and-white situations, when in reality they are much grayer. When it comes to righteousness, evangelicals tend to categorize people as polar opposites—either very bad or very good—because it's easier to put people into categories than it is to love them through the complexities of life. But we must be cured from our idealism. We must stop creating all-or-nothing categories. Was Samson godly or ungodly? Was King Solomon wise or unwise? Did the apostle Paul do what he wanted to do or what he didn't want to do? People are complicated, and the Bible shows it's possible to be godly and yet still do very ungodly stuff from time to time. In

> *What we need to do as a Christian community is take a collective vow to never give up on people.*

our judgmental spirits, we see people as "all" or "nothing" because it's easier to write people off than it is to love them through their ungodly moments. What we need to do as a Christian community is take a collective vow to never give up on people.

People are seldom saved when they are loved from a distance. People are typically saved when a friend introduces them to Christ. Certainly, the ministries that love people from a distance are valuable. Being a pastor in a larger church has value. Writing a book or a blog has value. A radio ministry can help many people hear the gospel. Yet here's the sequence: Those ministries typically plant seeds and water seeds. Those seeds ripen over time, and then, more times than not, God uses an "up close" person to make Christ personal in another person's life. Programs are fine—they're some of the vehicles God uses to help people along. But God uses *people* to change people.

We need to love people up close—and that means being involved in messy, complex, difficult-to-categorize lives. I've got a good friend, Jeff, who's been coming to Highpoint for more than ten years. He came to church originally because he wanted to support his wife and her desire to raise their children in church. Jeff still hasn't made a decision to trust Christ, even after more than a decade of hearing the gospel and seeing how love works. We've had amazingly deep conversations about Jesus all along the way. Jeff serves. He gives. He supports the overall ministry and direction of the church. He's a complex friend—and I love him dearly—and I haven't given up on him. Why? Because he's my friend. It's really that simple.

3. Living out a mission of love means love saves us—and others—from sin.

When we love people, why do we love them? What's actually going on in the midst of this love?

Well, we help save them *from* something, and we help save them *to* something. We save them *from* the wrath of God and often from their own actions and heart-attitudes of self-destruction. We help save them *to* eternal life, ultimately, and to living a life of love here and now. We do what we can do, so Jesus can do what only he can do.

It can be a tricky thing to understand the wrath of God. When we think of wrath, we often superimpose our human understanding and experiences of wrath onto God. If a person is filled with wrath, then that person is furious—stomping around the house, kicking and screaming, throwing things, calling people names. But that's not what God's wrath is like at all.

The Bible describes God's wrath as a positional sort of wrath. God is holy and must be separated from sin. So, in this sense, "wrath" is God's stance toward sin and disobedience. God's wrath is his righteous judgment toward evil. God himself took his wrath for us when Jesus died on the cross. God sent his own Son to pay the cost of our sin. Now, instead of us receiving the wrath of God, we are able to receive the righteousness of God. It's our privilege to be able to offer that gift of righteousness to other people so that nobody need experience the wrath of God.

This good news is found in 1 Thessalonians 5:9, "For God has not destined us for wrath, but to obtain salvation through our Lord Jesus Christ" (ESV). The core message of the gospel is that we were once enemies of God, but he reconciles us to himself through his Son, Jesus. Once there was a broken relationship between us and God, yet Jesus bridges that gap; he heals the relationship when we trust in him. Here's our purpose statement as active believers: "We become all things to all people, by all means, to save some from the wrath of God." The adoption of that statement keeps us focused and moving forward.

When we love people, we help save them from their own acts of self-destruction. This means that love can protect people from some of the effects of sin. Certainly not *all* the effects, for we live in a sinful world, and sometimes God allows the sin of

> *Every time we choose to love God and to love people, then love wins and sin loses.*

other people to influence us. But a life that follows Jesus is a life free from so many of sin's forms of entanglement and destruction. Sin is always a busybody, always looking for entry points. Sin never ceases to work. But love is the cure for sin. Love is the antidote. Every time we choose to love God and to love people, then love wins and sin loses.

A New Focus

Our mission of loving others helps save others from sin . . . but did you know our mission helps save us from sin too? The key to life, and life more abundant, is about loving others more than being loved. When we focus on our mission, things begin to fall into place.

If we are struggling with a sin, we often want to focus on the sin itself. Certainly there's a case for putting to death the desires of the flesh (Col. 3:5); meaning if a sin creeps up in our lives, then we don't give it space to breathe. But the key to defeating sin is to turn to God. We come to the cross of Christ, and Jesus provides the cleansing. The key to life is not loving sin less but loving God more.

> *The key to life is not loving sin less but loving God more.*

See, if we focus on the sin, then we tend to delay coming to God. We feel ashamed because of what we've done. Or we feel angry at ourselves because we aren't strong enough to turn away from the sin on our own. Sometimes we even feel powerful—we tell ourselves we can defeat sin by ourselves, but that typically leads to sin too. Most of us allow our sin to cause us to avoid God, or at least delay coming to him. But that's the exact opposite of God's desire and direction. Hebrews 4:16 says, "Let us then with confidence draw near to the throne of grace, that we may receive mercy and find grace to help in time of need" (ESV). Stop hesitating. Come confidently.

Our mission isn't to judge sinners, or condemn people, or tell people to clean themselves up so they can get right with God. Jesus offers people compassion without criticism, condemnation, or compromise. Jesus is the perfect combination of truth and love, grace upon grace. Our call in life is to introduce people to Jesus.

Our mission is to love. And one of the big ways we do that is to meet, befriend, and love people exactly where they are.

If you'd like to watch Josh and Stacie tell their story, go to ChrisConlee.net.

9

The Bowl and Towel

Love plays offense, not defense.

The leap from middle school to high school felt like jumping into a new world for Joshua Jenkins. It was a chance to step out of his comfort zone and remake himself, although he wasn't quite sure who to remake himself into. As first order of business, Joshua tried out for the football team at Overton High School and made it. This surprised him because he'd never been much of a football player before. He'd always been more of an artist. But this was only the first surprise he'd encounter during his high school years.

Joshua, who's African American, noticed that the football team at Overton had an unlikely group of supporters—a bunch of people from a church called Highpoint. Joshua was skeptical at first about these white Christians from another part of town showing up in the inner city. "We're accustomed to the white Christians showing up only once to serve," he said, "taking their do-good picture, and not showing up again until next year."

At the time, Joshua didn't consider himself much of a Christian, if at all. His family attended church but they were mostly cultural Christians, which is still fairly common in the South. Joshua said, "Following the Lord was something you did only when you were old and had nothing to live for. At least, that's how I saw it at the time."

Home life was rocky for Joshua too. His dad had encountered some difficult times and had stopped going to church altogether. All he did was work, and then he'd come home frustrated and tired. Joshua and his dad didn't see eye to eye on a lot of things. "It was like a weight was always on my dad," Joshua said.

The year Joshua joined the football team was a good year. We'd begun an outreach to Overton High School a year earlier, helping out at the high school any way we could. Our goal was pretty simple. We simply wanted to reach beyond the walls of the church and love people within the community. So, we coordinated meals for the Overton football team before all their games. The coaches wouldn't send the players home for dinner because 40 percent wouldn't return for the game, so these players were playing under the Friday Night Lights with their last meal being the school lunch. The need is beyond our comprehension in our inner city schools.

We sponsored a Fellowship of Christian Athletes club at the school. We offered tutoring and ACT preparation classes on Saturdays. On Thursday afternoons, one of our student leaders would give devotions for the football team.

Toward the end of every school year, our student ministries department took part in a camp in Florida called Big Stuf for any high school student who wanted to attend, and it was always a lot of fun. One year, while Joshua was still in high school, we raised enough funds to send the entire football team to a sports camp.

Joshua began to notice a few things about the Christians who served his high school. "I'd never seen anything quite like it," he said, "and I couldn't believe the amount of love they showed for our football team."

One thing led to another—in all the best ways. Joshua and one of his sisters went for tutoring. Then they listened to a devotion or two and found the talks surprisingly relevant and deep. "The leaders were transparent about their walks with Christ," he said. "They showed me a whole new level of Christianity—not a Christianity that's stuck between church walls, but a Christianity that's out in the community, out getting into the mess of people's lives." Joshua and his sister then attended a youth service at Highpoint and remarked between themselves how they couldn't quite believe there were students their age who actually wanted to follow the Lord.

The start of something great happened when Joshua and his sister won a trip to Big Stuf. At that camp, both he and his sister made decisions to follow Christ. When they came back to Memphis, they told their parents they'd decided to follow the Lord. The kids started attending Highpoint regularly, and they were welcomed with open arms and loved by all. Their decision had a ripple effect on their parents, and soon the parents started coming too. "On their first Sunday there, I looked down the row at my dad and he had tears in his eyes," Joshua said. "My parents felt welcomed, wanted, and even respected, and pretty soon we knew we'd found a church home as a family."

At our church, we encourage whoever's been most influential in your life to baptize you. Picture this: You are in the tank surrounded by family and friends. A video of your faith story is played, you are baptized, and the entire place erupts as the band kicks into high gear with celebration. Joshua and his sister decided to be baptized and had their parents baptize them. It proved an amazing experience. "My sister and I were overjoyed," Joshua said. "We couldn't stop crying. All our friends from Overton came, and they were all cheering us on. It just felt like life would never be the same."

Then—this was cool—Joshua's biggest prayer had been answered when his parents baptized him and Tashua. But then his parents, Harold and Teri Jenkins, placed their faith in Jesus and asked Joshua and Tashua to baptize them the very next Sunday. Talk about a celebration! It was off the charts. Joshua says, "The cloud over my dad's head was taken away. He wasn't discouraged anymore."

The whole family grew in the faith. Joshua's other sister, Keishua, was also saved. Joshua started learning leadership skills from our student leaders. Another student leader took Joshua under his wing and discipled him. Joshua wanted to give back, so he volunteered to serve on Sunday mornings in children's ministries. Highpoint was with him every step of the way.

When Joshua graduated from high school, he was the first in his family to go to college. While he was away from home, people from Highpoint stayed in contact through emails, texts, and letters. "I was really struggling in college at first," Joshua said, "but Mama Susan—I call her—sent me encouraging letters with all her favorite Scriptures. I still have those letters to this day."

Joshua did a summer internship at Highpoint and sensed the Lord was calling him to full-time ministry. The internship paved the way for Joshua to come on staff a few years later in the student ministries department. He focused on outreach to Overton High School—on weekends, they'd feed hot dogs and hamburgers to the kids. While working for the church, Joshua met a student ministry volunteer named Lacey. They became best friends, then were engaged, then got married. They held their wedding and reception at Highpoint.

Joshua's no longer working for our church, but even that's an exciting step of ministry for him. Joshua is fluent in Spanish, and he's working now for a different nonprofit agency in Memphis, one that's reaching Hispanic kids for Christ. Joshua himself is now engaging with a different culture. He's paying it forward by loving people different from him.

From my perspective, what's amazing to see is that years ago, when we first decided as a church to serve a high school, we didn't know what we were doing or what to expect in terms of fruit or a harvest. In the case of Joshua, here's a young man who was saved through that specific ministry, discipled through the ministry, came back to serve in the ministry, then was sent out from the ministry to love and serve other people. Through our ministry to Overton, Joshua became a strong, capable leader who is now reaping a spiritual harvest.

"The people of Highpoint were not scared to enter my family's brokenness," Joshua said. "They showed me the beauty of Jesus and they met me and my family exactly where we were. We were able to encounter God's grace in abundance and see that through Christ, we are truly free."

Inch by Inch

Question: How do we, as the people of God, love people in such a way that we can prove love never quits and never gives up? Answer: we can *engage* the culture instead of *escape* the culture.

Ministering to the students and staff in a public school isn't an easy ministry. In the nine-plus years we've been working with Overton, only thirty to forty students total have chosen to trust Christ. By comparison, in just the past ten weeks at Highpoint, we've had nearly five hundred people make first-time decisions to follow Jesus. So, we need to ask if the time and resources spent at Overton are effectively used. I would say yes for many unexpected reasons. Obviously, all ministry is valuable, but we receive far more than we give in our ministry to Overton High School. The students and families at Overton aren't our outreach program; they are our family and friends. This is important in every city, but this is especially important in Memphis. Historically, we're a city that's more known for our racism and hatred than for our unity and love. This is precisely why those forty students in nine years are so significant. They have helped pave the way for us to become a church of diversity. Our vision was never *Let's go reach "white" Memphis*; our vision was, and is, *Let's go reach Memphis*.

As Christians, we need to be great at what matters most—loving God and loving people. And sometimes, when we look at the biblical commandments to love other people, we forget to love people who aren't like us. It's far easier to love people who talk the same as us, act the same as us, and have the same education and economic level and faith as us. But we see all the time in Scripture that Jesus loved people different from him—and he encourages us to do the same. Compassion moves us beyond comfort, convenience, and cost. Compassion is love at work—and work is not always comfortable or convenient.

> *Compassion moves us beyond comfort, convenience, and cost. Compassion is love at work—and work is not always comfortable or convenient.*

In Acts 17:16–34, the apostle Paul went to visit the city of Athens—and showed us a strong model of how to love people different from us. Paul was a Roman Jew, a follower of Christ. Athens was a Greek city, a large city even back then, and one enmeshed in idolatry. Statues of idols were all over the place, and the Athenians considered themselves extremely devout people.

Paul walked around the city for a while, just observing the people and taking notes on what he saw. Then he hiked over to the Areopagus, a prominent rock outcropping often called "Mars Hill," and gave a speech. The city court and other government functions were held at Mars Hill, and it was used as a place where the people in the city and influential thinkers of the day gathered and exchanged ideas. The modern equivalent of speaking at Mars Hill would be like Paul going on CNN.

Let's look at the speech he gave. He started by saying, "Men of Athens, I perceive that in every way you are very religious" (Acts 17:22 ESV).

This beginning is noteworthy for what Paul *didn't* say. Paul didn't start off by criticizing his listeners, as some Christians are prone to do. He didn't walk in and say, "Hey, men of Athens—you've got it all wrong. You're worshiping idols, and God hates that, and you're all going to go to hell!" No. He established a connection with the people as his first order of business. Even complimented them on their devotion and fervor. Do we do this with the people we encounter? Or are we quick to criticize them for ungodliness—to insist we are right and they are wrong? Do we seek to build connections, to have genuine friendships, to truly serve and love people in the best possible way?

In far too many ways, Christians have lost our voice in the world today because we have shouted in criticism rather than acted with compassion.

This is particularly important whenever Christians dip into politics. The Right criticizes the Left, and the Left criticizes the Right. Christians become entangled with both sides, hot-button topics are pushed, and we Christians become known more for who we hate rather than who we love. This should not be. In far too many ways, Christians have lost our voice in the world today because we have shouted in criticism rather than acted with compassion. We have debated people instead of loving people, and we have condemned people rather than pointing them toward the glory of God.

Paul continued in his speech: "For as I passed along and observed the objects of your worship, I found also an altar with this inscription: 'To the unknown god.' What therefore you worship as unknown, this I proclaim to you" (Acts 17:23 ESV).

The Athenians were so careful in their religious fervor to serve all the idols of their day and age that they wanted to make sure they didn't leave any unnoticed. They had an idol to Zeus, and an idol to Aphrodite, an idol to Achilles, and all the rest of the 683 Greek deities. And then the Athenians even set up an idol to an unknown god in case they'd missed one. The bridge that Paul began to establish was to make "the unknown God" known to them.

Paul said, "The God who made the world and everything in it, being Lord of heaven and earth, does not live in temples made by man, nor is he served by human hands, as though he needed anything, since he himself gives to all mankind life and breath and everything" (vv. 24–25 ESV).

That's the God we serve. Paul simply laid out the facts. This unknown God gives life and breath to everything. He doesn't need to dwell in temples because he's the owner of heaven and earth. Paul pointed people to God. He described who God is and what he's like.

Then Paul made a surprising move. He wove in bits of the Athenians' own arts and literature along with his definition of God.

> And he made from one man every nation of mankind to live on all the face of the earth, having determined allotted periods and the boundaries of their dwelling place, that they

should seek God, and perhaps feel their way toward him and find him. Yet he is actually not far from each one of us, for

"In him we live and move and have our being";

as even some of your own poets have said,

"For we are indeed his offspring." (Acts 17:26–28 ESV)

Do you catch what's happening? In order to connect with pagans, Paul read the poetry of pagans. He immersed himself enough in the culture of unbelievers to be fluent in what mattered most to them. Paul had studied the culture of nonbelievers—and he used that culture as a reference point to tell them about Jesus.

Then Paul got more specific. He told them about the resurrection.

Being then God's offspring, we ought not to think that the divine being is like gold or silver or stone, an image formed by the art and imagination of man. The times of ignorance God overlooked, but now he commands all people everywhere to repent, because he has fixed a day on which he will judge the world in righteousness by a man whom he has appointed; and of this he has given assurance to all by raising him from the dead. (vv. 29–31 ESV)

Paul's logic was this: If humans are the children of God, then the children of God should reflect the image of God because children should resemble their father. Since that's the case, children shouldn't take earthly substances such as gold and silver and stone and project those earthly things back onto God, because that's not how things work. The sequence is wrong. God had overlooked this error in the past, but now God was calling all people to turn from their error.

Yep, Paul actually used the word *repent* when talking to the Athenians—and I know that *repent* can be an emotionally charged word these days, but it simply means to change our minds. Paul encouraged the people of his day to change their minds about who the unknown God was.

Those were bold statements of Paul's, and it's okay for us to make bold statements too. When we interact with the world today, we can be too cautious, too concessionary, too cloaked in our language. Sometimes we need to be overt and clear in our speech, not guarded or metaphoric. We need to tell people exactly who Jesus is, point out his wonder and goodness, and invite people to celebrate with us how Jesus brings us back to God and gives us new hearts and new lives.

The proof that Paul offered the Athenians was the resurrection of Christ. Certainly, there's a time and place for walking people through intricate proofs of the faith, for the art and science of apologetics, for offering people detailed studies that prove the existence of God and the reliability of the Bible. Yet at other times, we simply need to point people to the resurrection of Jesus and talk about that. Why is this important? Because the leaders of every other religion in the world are all dead. Abraham and Moses are dead. Confucius is dead. Mohammed is dead. Buddha is dead.

But Jesus isn't dead! The Son of God has defeated sin and death forever. Jesus was crucified on a Roman cross. He truly died—the soldiers pierced his side but didn't break his legs, which they would have done if he wasn't dead. Jesus was placed in a guarded and sealed tomb. Then that tomb was discovered empty. Jesus was raised on the third day according to the Scriptures. He appeared to Peter, and then to the disciples, and after that, he appeared to more than five hundred people (1 Cor. 15:3–6).

That's the proof Paul offered. Jesus is alive!

Here's how the Athenians responded:

> Now when they heard of the resurrection of the dead, some mocked. But others said, "We will hear you again about this." So Paul went out from their midst. But some men joined him and believed, among whom also were Dionysius the Areopagite and a woman named Damaris and others with them. (Acts 17:32–34 ESV)

Some people sneered. Some people were curious and wanted to hear more at a later date. And some people believed.

Isn't that always the way it works? When we tell people about Jesus, some people won't want to hear it. Others will feel curious, even encouraged, and hopefully, will want to hear more. This is a win. When we share Christ with people, we can't just shove Christ down people's throats. We need to leave them wanting to hear more. A relationship is built inch by inch, not mile by mile.

And others will believe. Right away, their hearts and lives will be changed by Christ.

The Bowl and Towel

We often hear as Christians that we are to "be in the world but not of the world"—and this is true, this is how the Bible teaches us to live. But what does it actually mean?

If we are "in" the world, then we are immersed in the culture of the world. We interact with people who don't know God. We live as Jesus lived, not sequestered away by himself, safe from any and all messy people, but regularly interacting with people who needed to be reconciled to God. Jesus said, "I have come into the world as light, so that whoever believes in me may not remain in darkness" (John 12:46 ESV).

If we are "of" the world, then that means we love the things of the world that stand contrary to God. We are *not* to be this way. First John 2:15–16 says, "Do not love the world or the things in the world. . . . For all that is in the world—the desires of the flesh and the desires of the eyes and pride of life—is not from the Father but is from the world" (ESV).

So, we are to be immersed in the culture of the world, yet we are not to love that which is contrary to God. But have you ever noticed how we Christians tend to fall into one camp but not the other? We're either so immersed in the world that we're tempted toward worldly living, or we're so far removed from the world that the only people we know are other Christians. This should not be. In other places in this book, I encourage us to be strong in Christ and to overcome temptations toward worldly living—in other words, to be not of the world. So, what I want to do in the remainder of this chapter is to encourage us to be in the world. We need to be strong enough in Christ that we can be friends with people who aren't Christians.

See, the problem is we remove ourselves from the world and create our own subculture. We create Christian books and Christian music and Christian movies and Christian magazines and Christian schools and Christian gyms and Christian websites and Christian cruises and Christian bowling alleys and Christian theme parks—and all of these are fine, if we understand their purpose is mostly to encourage Christians and train Christians. But if we're not careful, we can spend all our time immersed in this Christian subculture. Listen—our goal is not separation from the world. Our goal is not security. Our goal is *not* to play defense. Our goal is to play offense. To carry the ball forward toward the goal line. We "press on toward the goal to win the prize for which God has called [us] heavenward in Christ Jesus" (Phil. 3:14).

I realize it's not always fun to engage with the culture around us. The culture can be messy and dirty and even dangerous. But if the church only strives to escape the culture, then the church will become powerless. We don't want power in the sense that we want to govern the world or become the captains of industry—that's not the type of power I'm talking about. The power lies in changed hearts and changed lives. Why must we engage the culture? Because the gospel always "goes." The gospel *moves*. It acts, it runs, it speaks. We can't simply cluster inside our churches and hope that people will come to church. We must throw open the doors of the church and go out into the world. We must *be* the church outside of the walls of the church, and to do that we need to simply be real people committed to reaching real people in the reality of our fallen and broken world.

Far too many non-Christians come away feeling unworthy, unwanted, and unwelcomed when they encounter Christians. We will never win people to Christ by making them feel this way. We need to make non-Christians feel welcome. We don't win people by criticizing them. We win people by connecting with them, by listening to them, by finding genuine ways to compliment them. We don't have to agree with all the things in their lives, but the point is that we can continually find ways to build bridges.

Our approach to people can determine if they will receive us or not, and our approach needs to be led by love. If we lead with truth, then the truth will often come across as too harsh. People will not want the truth right away. But if we love people first, then they will receive the truth in time, as the Holy Spirit works in their lives.

Think of it this way: the most dominant symbol of Christianity today is the cross. We see crosses inside and outside church buildings. People wear crosses around their necks as a sign of their faith. Sometimes people will put a little cross beside their name and address on their business card to let others know they're Christians. And there's certainly nothing wrong with the symbol of the cross.

But there's also another symbol of Christianity—and this symbol is one I wish more of us would embrace. It's the symbol of the bowl and towel. This symbol memorializes when Jesus washed his disciples' feet. It's the symbol of service. "Whoever wants to become great among you must be your servant," Jesus told his disciples (Mark 10:43). If we never use the bowl and towel in our interactions with others, then people will never embrace the cross.

Are we serving people—truly serving people—in love?

You and the World

Why serve people in love? Because love works. Love works when nothing else works. Love works because love covers a multitude of sins. Love works because love never fails.

So, here comes the controversial part of this chapter, okay? God's truth isn't always safe truth, and what I want to do is put some flesh on these ideas and offer a few specific examples of what it might look like to be in the world and not of the world. Keep in mind that different people have different specific callings, so not every scenario will fit every person—and that's okay.

Love works when nothing else works. Love works because love covers a multitude of sins. Love works because love never fails.

Non-Christians are going to act like non-Christians. Our calling isn't to criticize non-Christians for participating in their sins of choice. "What business is it of mine to judge those outside the church?" (1 Cor. 5:12). Our calling is to love non-Christians, serve them, be their friends, and then start talking to them about the "unknown God," because he is life and breath.

Have I offended you yet?

I hope not. Let's talk about some specific examples. All of us as parents want to teach our children how to be discerning. We want them to know what's right and what's wrong. We want them to walk that narrow walk where they protect their mind and guard their heart, yet still know how to engage the culture. We want them to be friends with children their age who aren't Christians, and we want our children to be able to talk with their non-Christian friends about whatever kids talk about these days—and to do so from a place of wisdom and discernment so they can love their friends and introduce their friends to Christ.

Certainly, there are some things we don't want our children to see or do. Certainly, there are movies and TV shows and songs and video games that are complete trash. And certainly, there's a whole lot of secular culture that falls somewhere in between. It's not all good, but it's not all bad, either. What do we do, then?

Well, we need to serve the Lord—period. And that takes discernment of our own. Some families will make the case that we can best serve the Lord by cutting ourselves off from every gray area of culture—and if that's the decision you make, then I want to respect that. But other families will make the case that the best way we can serve the Lord is by teaching our children discernment, encouraging our children to have some friends who aren't Christians, and praying like mad that our children will be immersed in the lives of their non-Christian friends and will help lead them a step closer to Jesus. If a movie isn't over the top, and our kids want to see a movie, then maybe it's okay to see it—and then go for pizza and discuss what was wise and unwise in the movie. Instead of thinking for our children, we teach them how to think for themselves.

Is it difficult to engage the culture for the sake of Christ? Yes. Is it dangerous to engage the culture? Sometimes. Will Christians make mistakes along the way? Yes.

But—and I want to say this point loudly—it's also dangerous to *escape* the culture.

See, I'd prefer to take the risk that Mark and Annika, my children, would become sinners rather than Pharisees. In fact, they are already sinners because we are all sinners. The good news is sinners can see their need for Christ and sinners can be redeemed and forgiven. But the Pharisees were like whitewashed graves—shiny and clean to look at, but full of death inside. They mistakenly thought they became righteous by keeping rules and separating themselves from messy people. They looked down their noses at other people and prided themselves on being better than everybody else. And Jesus reserved his harshest words for Pharisees. He called them blind guides, fools, snakes, and hypocrites.

As a parent, I want to take my chances by engaging with the culture. I'd rather teach my children how to fight the good fight than run from the battle. The way we do this as parents is to teach our children to love God more, not love sin less. We can preach to our kids until we're blue in the face about the dangers of alcohol and drugs and premarital sex. But when we teach them to love God more— and they actually learn how to love God more—then they're automatically going to love sin less.

When we teach them to love God more— and they actually learn how to love God more—then they're automatically going to love sin less.

How about this? In recent years, we've witnessed an incredible clash of cultures between the LGBTQ community and the Christian community. It's turned into a real "us versus them" mentality—and that's just wrong. There's a perception that gays are hated by Christians, and that's just horrible, absolutely horrible. If you go get your hair cut, and you find out the barber is gay, and you say "I don't want to go back there," then who's going to love that person in the name of Jesus? Go build a friendship with your barber. Go prove that love works. Remember, our actions speak louder than our words.

Or this? In your office at work, maybe everybody quits for the day and goes down to the bar to relax. They've invited you, but you've said no because that's not what you do. If you're in recovery as an alcoholic, then that's fine, don't go to the bar. But what if you went down to the bar with your non-Christian coworkers because you genuinely love them? You build friendships with them, little by little. You ask questions and let them talk about their lives. You hear their stories and begin to understand what makes them tick. You don't need to drink if you don't want to. Go have a Diet Coke or a mug of coffee. But if you aren't engaging with them, then who will love your coworkers for the sake of Jesus?

You say your testimony will be ruined if you go into a bar? Remember that Jesus was known as "a friend of sinners" (Luke 7:34). People who live in darkness don't like the light, and they're not going to come to church to hear about Jesus. So, we must go to them because the gospel always goes. I'm not giving you license to sin; I'm giving you license to go to sinners. Certainly, there's risk, but too many of us are focused on the risk and not the reward. The reward is building the friendship and carrying the gospel and one day hearing from Jesus, "Well done, good and faithful servant."

> *We must go to them because the gospel always goes. I'm not giving you license to sin; I'm giving you license to go to sinners.*

Our mission is to love people; it's to carry to people the love found in one of the most famous passages of Scripture, John 3:16: "For God so loved the world, that He gave His only begotten Son, that whoever believes in Him shall not perish, but have eternal life" (NASB).

Who does God love?

The world.

That's what I want all of us to do too. I want us to quit playing defense and start playing offense. I want us to stop protecting ourselves and start risking for the sake of the gospel. I want us to follow the example of Jesus and engage the culture, not escape the culture.

And I want us to do this because love works.

Does this feel scary to you? Do you get a knot in your gut when you think about engaging the world with love? The great news is there's incredible joy for us when love works. Joy! Not fear. Joy! Not anxiousness.

If you'd like to watch Joshua tell his
story, go to ChrisConlee.net.

10

Wealthy Traditions for the Rest of Us

Love ain't easy, but love brings joy.

You don't need to be a theologian or a super-Christian in order to love well. The late Bill and Ann Willard were acutely aware of that. They were middle class folks, salt of the earth type Christians who simply loved their family and community with all they had. They both finished life well. I had the privilege of presiding over one of their funerals and participating in the other, and they both left behind a tremendous legacy of love. Bill died April 29, 2014, at age seventy-five, and Ann died two years later, on May 18, 2016, at age seventy-six. They'd been married since 1958, and both of their funerals were celebrations in every respect, full of laughter, not tears. Their lives were rich testimonies of proving love works.

As a pastor, one of the most special and powerful things I've ever witnessed was when I visited Ann a day or two before she died. I lingered in the hospital room and watched all five of her children come to say goodbye to her. They didn't know how much longer she had, but knew the end was close. She looked each of her children in the eyes and said, "You've made me proud." It was so great to see. At both Ann's and Bill's funerals, I talked about how true success is achieved when the people closest to you know and feel your love the most. There was no denying that love worked in this family.

Altogether, the Willards had four boys and one girl, and I invited their oldest son, Bill ("Bull"), to tell a snippet of their family's story in his own words:

My parents would be astounded and humbled to think anyone would be impressed by their lives, or that part of their story would be featured in a book. The thing they were always most proud of was their kids and their grandkids. That's how they lived—always loving their family.

Daddy was always available to us as kids. He was always willing to talk with us, always willing to spend time with us, always accessible. He was always helpful, advising us, listening to us vent—whatever was needed.

He and Mom were perfect together. She was like a character in *Steel Magnolias*, a staunch defender of her children, always in love. You always knew Mom had your back. Once, not too long before she passed, she even chewed out a referee for fouling out her grandbaby in a basketball game. Her nickname was "Hurricane," and when she died, all my friends changed their social media bio pictures to a hurricane.

Daddy met Mom when he was thirteen and she was eleven. Daddy was roofing a shed, and Mom came by in shorts. Daddy took one look, fell off the shed, and landed on the sidewalk. They always laughed whenever they told that story. They grew up together and never ever dated anyone else. Daddy graduated from high school and went into the Navy. Some other guy tried to date her when Daddy was out of town, so he came home, declared his intent, and it was all over. As soon as Mom graduated, they tied the knot. She was eighteen when they married, and he was twenty.

After Daddy finished up in the Navy, he worked for the Federal Aviation Administration as an electronics technician and later as a supervisor. He retired early, then went and taught college-level electronics and computer programming for several years and loved that. Daddy turned down promotions at work while we were in school because he always wanted us to have a home base, and he considered his children too important to uproot.

Mom never worked outside the house. It was important to both her and Daddy that she was at home for us. If we kids had a date, Mom would wait up for us. Sometimes she'd have fallen asleep on the couch, and I'd come in and kiss her on the cheek to wake her up. She was always there for us if we needed to talk. I can't tell you how many breakups that woman talked us all through.

We were never rich as a family, but we always had enough. None of us felt like we ever lacked anything. We lived in a three bedroom, one-and-a-half bathroom house. Our sister Melanie had a room to herself, Mom and Dad had a room, Richie and Lanny (the two youngest boys) had a room to themselves, and then Daddy made a room in the garage for me and Scott. The reason we didn't lack anything wasn't because of money but because of love. Our parents both lived by the idea that love for their family was the most important thing. Love is free, yet it's the most valuable commodity we have, and one of our parents' big legacies is that they redefined wealth for our family.

Daddy gave us all nicknames. I was Bubba. Melanie was Sissy. Scott was Scott-bird (this was during the Lyndon Johnson years), Lanny was Lanny-Bo, and Richie was Richie-Bo. We kids all played sports growing up, and my parents never missed a ballgame—not for us, and not for the grandchildren, either, when they came along. When I was eighteen, I was playing softball, and our team needed a coach. We couldn't play in the league without one. Daddy had never coached softball, but that didn't stop him from saying yes. He was left-handed, and if we were ever short of a player, he'd catch for us, using someone else's glove. The last season he coached us, we bought him a left-handed glove, and he got teary-eyed. He was always encouraging the team any way he could. At Daddy's funeral, almost all the players who'd been on that team showed up to pay their respects. We were all fifty-year-old men by then, but we remembered the love Daddy had showed our team.

When we kids were older and married, Mom and Daddy never thought of our spouses as "in-laws." They became the same as their own kids, and Daddy and Mom introduced our spouses as their daughters and sons too. This was never to the degradation of the relationship our spouses had with their own parents. It was just how Daddy and Mom thought of them. We'd ask Mom and Daddy for input and advice, and they'd give it to us, but they'd always tell our spouses to seek advice from their own parents too. About a year before Mom passed, I went down to the rest home and picked her up for a birthday dinner. I picked up my wife's mom, too, and the first things my mother said to my mother-in-law when she saw her were "I love you" and "I miss you."

Our friends were always welcome in our house, and my parents always made sure to know our friends' names and make them feel welcome. We had a lot of family traditions. Having family dinners together was one of the most important traditions. Even after we grew up and left the house, many of these traditions continued. We kids would often show up at Daddy and Mom's place after work, and a couple nights a week we'd all have dinner together. The grandkids would go there after school and get snacks.

A few years before Daddy passed, he and Mom went on a trip to Mt. Rushmore and around the States to see all the places they'd always wanted to see. In case anything happened to them on the trip, Daddy typed out a letter beforehand. It read, in part: "We love you all, all our kids and their spouses, and the grandkids. You've made us very proud. Even though we've never had much money, you've always made us feel wealthy."

Traditions have a way of playing out in the next generation. After I left the house, I got into the habit of calling Daddy every day on my way home from work just to say hello and talk. I did that for years and years, and when Daddy died, my drive home became one of the hardest things for me because I missed him so much. My son Cody is twenty-nine now, and he found out about this. Well, guess who calls me every afternoon on his drive home? Cody calls me like clockwork.

When you're growing up, you think your parents are immortal. When Daddy died, it came as a surprise because he'd always been a strong man in good health. He'd had strep throat but didn't realize it, and died of sepsis. What made his passing particularly hard was seeing Mom after

Daddy died. She missed him so much. One of the things that got her through the next two years was she felt she needed to be there for us for a while—she told us that. She had non-Hodgkin's lymphoma and beat it, but then she ended up dying of complications caused by the cancer. Neither of our folks were scared of dying. They both said, "I know where I'll be, and I'll know Who I'll be with."

After Daddy and Mom died, all the grandkids told us not to stop getting together, so the whole family continues to gather regularly. The grandkids range in age from one year old to thirty-two, and they're a tight group; they love and care for each other. There's no fear that our family will separate or break. We've been passed the baton of love, and now we're passing it along to our kids. We have confidence that we'll build on the legacy that was established for us.

As a family, we all know that love works.

Three Responses to Love

Wow, I hope my kids can say that about our family after I'm gone! I want to be a great husband and father and friend to others, consistently leading with love in my interactions with people. Bill and Ann Willard served our church in countless ways. Emma, one of their granddaughters, is now on staff. Everyone who knew them noted the great love they had for their family. They redefined wealth—and they didn't leave their kids a legacy of money. Their children want to be around each other. Their grandchildren want to be around each other. It's great to see that Bill and Ann's legacy continues today. It's more than a legacy of love; it's also a legacy of joy.

That's one of the clearest results of the gospel working. And that's what we want to talk about in this chapter—a legacy of joy that's prompted by love. I realize this book is titled *Love Works* and we're focusing on the second word in that title quite a bit—*works*—and work isn't associated with joy much of the time. But did you know there's incredible joy for us when love works? It's not a duty to love others. It's not drudgery to love others. It's not a sweat-filled, pickax-style work to love others. It's a joyful kind of work.

We minimize joy too much in Christianity. We might sing about it at Christmastime, but most of us don't pray for joy in our lives on a daily basis. We think that's selfish or unimportant, but we are mistaken. It precisely describes Jesus' purpose toward us. In John 15:11, Jesus describes his ministry as *full of joy*, saying, "These things I have spoken to you, that my joy may be in you, and that your joy may be full" (ESV).

Notice two very important words in this verse: "my" and "your." Jesus didn't come to teach us how to earn his joy. Jesus came to give us his joy. The words "my joy" demand that we ask this question: What was the joy of Jesus? It's important to know the answer because that's what he is giving us. He's not giving us *our definition* of joy. He is giving us *his* joy.

Jesus' joy involved two key components. First is the joy of being the Son of God. When Jesus gives us that part of his joy, it's the joy that comes from us becoming a child of God, a son or daughter of the King. Second is the joy of doing the work of God. Jesus' joy came from his relationship with his Father first and pleasing his Father second. Jesus didn't try to please his Father to earn the relationship;

rather, he desired to please his Father because he already had the relationship. The *who* always comes before the *what*. That's joy!

And notice the second part of verse 11: "that your joy may be full." How is our joy made full? It's made full by doing what Jesus did. It's made full by leading people to experience the gift of love that restores us to a right relationship with the Father. Our joy is never more full than when we see God's love work in others.

Joy is not a temporary emotion that makes us laugh or chuckle, and then we feel something else. The truest experience of joy isn't generated by an amusement park ride or a birthday party or even a big achievement. It's not a temporary sense of merriment. Rather, true joy is the deep sense of abiding satisfaction we get when we're in a right relationship with God the Father. When this relationship is set, then we can develop this positive cycle of receiving joy and giving joy. The more joy we receive, the more joy we give.

Joy was never meant to be complicated. What did Jesus say? "These things I have spoken to you, that MY joy may be IN YOU, and that YOUR joy may be FULL." Again, what is Jesus' joy? It's being the apple of the Father's eye. Is there any better picture of joy than a Father making his child smile, giggle, or laugh in his arms? It brings joy to the Father to give joy to his child, and it brings joy to the child to give joy to his father. Since Jesus has received the greatest gift in the world—being loved by a good, good Father—then he naturally wants to give that gift to us. There's no greater joy than giving the greatest gift. This is precisely why the joy of Christmas isn't about receiving gifts as much as it is about giving gifts. There's always joy in receiving, but there's always more joy in giving.

If you've been a Christian for a while, this may sound like old hat to you. Or maybe it sounds too deep theologically and feels irrelevant to your life. I don't want us to run by this too quickly. It's too important. Think of it this way. Imagine that one of your primary relationships is out of harmony. Maybe there's tension between you and your spouse. Between you and your child. You and your best friend. You and your boss. What does life feel like when it's out of harmony like that? It's tense, isn't it? If you don't have harmony in your main relationships, then nothing in the world feels right until that harmony is restored.

That's what life feels like when you don't have Christ. Maybe you wouldn't articulate the tension exactly this way, but if you don't have Christ, then there's a big emptiness in your life, a void in your heart. You'll always be searching, always be longing, always feel empty. You'll constantly be searching for fulfillment in things and people and events that you hope will satisfy you, but nothing will feel right until your relationship with God is restored through Jesus Christ. If you're already a Christian, then have you forgotten what life was like before you had Christ? If you've faithfully walked the path, have you forgotten what it's like to live with despair and darkness and a constant sense of searching? Have you forgotten how much you needed forgiveness?

When the barrier of emptiness between you and God is taken down, then joy springs into existence. The void is filled. You feel this incredible relief. You and God were never meant to be separated from one another. Your joy is restored because your relationship is restored. Something was missing until you reconciled. Something will always be missing without the relationship. Only Jesus can fill the emptiness in your heart, but once it is filled, then your greatest joy is giving his joy to others.

My children, Mark and Annika, don't need to earn my love. I am their father and they always have my love, even if they disobey me or displease me. My love is not conditional for them. They don't need to be afraid they'll ever lose it. Even if they do something wrong—I still love them. Even if they turn their back on me—I still love them. This love exists because of the relationship. My love for them never changes, but the joy depends on the quality of our relationship and the quality of their relationships with others. Ultimately, joy is the fruit of God's love in me and through me. All of us experience joy when we are the recipient of love, but receiving only is temporary. God never designed for his love to stop with us but rather to flow through us. The joy comes from watching faith, hope, and love flourish along the banks of the river.

From Receiving to Responding

Here's a twist on salvation. When we receive the gift of God's love, all is made well, yet Christ calls us to go deeper in our relationship with him. There's more to the Christian life than just receiving. There's responding. Christ's invitation to us is to abide in his love. This is a biblical concept, this "abide," and it's found all through John 15 where Jesus compares himself to a vine and the Father to a gardener.

When we "abide" with Christ it means we remain with him, we continue with him, we stay close to him, and we reside in him. We are like branches on the vine and we continually stay close to the source of life, the vine. The gardener cares for us as branches, always working in love to make the branches more fruitful. The key to staying in God's love is responding to God's love.

This concept of "responding" to Christ's love bears closer examination because that's always what every parent hopes to receive from their child—response. Have you ever seen a spoiled child? Or maybe a young adult who feels entitled is better imagery. You can picture it. You can't stand the spoiled young adult because he's receiving love but he's not responding to that love. He's taking and taking from his parents, but he's giving nothing in return. A love relationship is a two-way relationship, and the relationship can't progress, develop, and mature if it's in the "receiving only" category. The relationship begins to thrive only when it goes from receiving to responding.

> *A love relationship is a two-way relationship, and the relationship can't progress, develop, and mature if it's in the "receiving only" category.*

As I love Mark and Annika, I always hope they respond to my love with their own love in return. They don't need to respond to ensure my love—my love is always there. But I simply enjoy their responses. Their responses let me know they're living in light of my love. Their responses let me know they're maturing in life. As children of God, that's how it works for us and God. We respond to God not out of duty but out of delight. Not because we have to but because we want to. Not because it's a rule but because it's a relationship—and that relationship is maturing. When someone loves me, my most natural and normal response is to love them back.

What might a response look like? Let's put it back into the sphere of Mark and Annika with Karin and me, using our family as a metaphor of how we love God. Children can respond to their parents in at least three ways.

First, if I tell them that I love them, and they say "I love you" back to me, that pretty much makes my heart burst. As a parent, I'm continually pouring love into my children. It would be devastating if Mark or Annika never loved me back. Certainly, they've had seasons of responding this way more than at other times. But I'm assured that my children love me—and it thrills me every single time to hear it. How do I know? I immediately worry if I don't hear it.

Second, if I do something for my children in love, and if they respond with gratitude by thanking me, then that's also a hope of mine. When my children are grateful, they gain a glimpse of how much Karin and I have sacrificed for them over the years. We don't require gratitude from our children. But it's nice to receive it, that's for sure. If our children fall into the pattern of only receiving from us without being grateful in return, then we get concerned for them. We fear they're spoiled, and nobody admires or respects a spoiled child. We all want to see grateful children.

> As a parent, I know that my children's joy in life doesn't depend on doing everything right but on how well they love others.

Third, perhaps best of all, if I do something for my children in love, and then they turn around and do a similar thing for someone else—that's also my desire. It shows they are learning how to love others. And it shows they are walking the path of life the best way they can—by receiving love and letting it flow through them so they love others. As a parent, I know that my children's joy in life doesn't depend on doing everything right but on how well they love others. The ultimate form of security and stability for my children depends on the health of their relationships. They must know not only how to receive love but how to respond and give love back. Joy comes from loving others well.

The Hour Has Come

What kinds of things bring spiritual joy in our lives?

Luke 15:10 contains one of the biggest answers to this question. Jesus says, "I tell you, there is joy before the angels of God over one sinner who repents" (ESV). Joy occurs when people follow the Lord. Even the angels witness and experience joy. If you want joy in your church, then start bringing people to Jesus. When people come to Jesus, they're spiritual babies—and nothing causes more joy than a baby. Lots of love equals lots of babies. Actually, come to think of it, *no love* equals *no babies* too. And that's the common denominator with joyless churches—they've stopped seeing spiritual babies being born.

In physical life, nothing compares to the joy that happens when your first child is born. I was there when both Mark and Annika were born, and I can tell you that the joy factor is overwhelming. The kid can't even do much as a baby. All a baby does is cry, eat, and poop. But in an instant, your love is endless and selfless. Your child is first, and you come second. You live for the joy of your child.

This is precisely what Jesus does for us. In John 16:16–21, Jesus told his disciples that he was going to the cross soon, and then after that he would be resurrected. The disciples had a hard time comprehending the totality of Jesus' words. He said to them, "You will be sorrowful, but your sorrow will turn into joy" (v. 20 ESV). He knew they were going to be devastated when he died, but he gave them hope beyond the grave.

See, they didn't understand that the resurrection was coming. They'd left everything to follow Jesus. They lived in a day and time when the Jewish people were constantly looking for the Messiah. They put their hope in Jesus, and many of them misunderstood what the kingdom of God was all about. It wasn't an earthly kingdom filled with literal thrones and swords and power, but rather a spiritual kingdom filled with compassion and joy and being reconciled to God. Jesus told them about dying and about the resurrection, and he told them this with much authority. It was a declaration: "Your sorrow will turn into joy."

Then Jesus gave his disciples a powerful illustration that undergirds everything we know of joy. Jesus said, "When a woman is giving birth, she has sorrow because her hour has come, but when she has delivered the baby, she no longer remembers the anguish, for joy that a human being has been born into the world" (John 16:21 ESV). That's joy.

Do you see the parallel? There's something amazing about pregnancy. You dread the hour, but you also can't wait for the hour. That's exactly how it was when Karin had Mark, our firstborn—there was sorrow at first, but the sorrow turned into joy. Karin labored naturally until "her hour came," and when that hour came, Karin literally asked the doctor: "If I get an epidural, do I still get the baby?" The doctor said yes, and Karin shouted, "GIVE ME THE EPIDURAL!" It was the most authoritative statement I've ever heard her make! Karin had sorrow because her hour had come, but then she had joy because the joy of her baby was set before her. The anguish was gone! The joy surpassed the sorrow because the joy was greater than the sorrow.

Jesus endured the hour of the cross to give us life. His hour came, and he did not relish the thought of taking hell for us on the cross. He prayed that the cup would be removed from him. But he also relished the Father's will. Jesus' hour came, and there was no stopping his hour. The baby was coming and nothing was going to stop that baby! Jesus looked forward to the joy that came when he pleased the Father, the joy of being fully sufficient to bring God's children home, the joy that his Father gives to all of us. Then the anguish was gone!

That's joy. The "baby" of sonship is with us today. The joy of new birth is available to us, and we can't push joy back in! Jesus labored in pain and his labor pains couldn't be stopped, but now a baby is born. The work of Christ is finished. He has sat down at the right hand of the Father, and God's children can now be in a right relationship with the Father. That's where all our joy springs from.

We are sons and daughters of the living God!

Full Joy for You Today

Let's talk some more about sorrow being turned to joy. This is so great, we can't miss it.

In John 17, Jesus earnestly prays for his disciples—and this includes me and you, too, if you follow Jesus. This specific prayer took place between the events of the Last Supper and Jesus' betrayal in the Garden of Gethsemane, and it beautifully sums up Jesus' relationship with his disciples. For us, the gospel is about salvation, being restored to God, and the Christian life is about sanctification, being gradually changed more and more into the image of Christ. John 17 talks about both salvation and sanctification, and does so with the overarching umbrella of joy in mind.

Jesus prays, "Now this is eternal life: that they know you, the only true God, and Jesus Christ, whom you have sent" (John 17:3). That's the salvation process explained—that we would know God, and that we would know God through Jesus Christ. Eternal life is being in a relationship with God. Listen: it's impossible for us to meet the resurrected Christ and not have joy.

Then, in verse 13, Jesus prays, "I am coming to you now, but I say these things while I am still in the world, so that they may have the full measure of my joy within them." This is the sanctification process explained. It's Jesus' purpose in our lives. His joy is made full in us. Jesus died to forgive us from our sin (salvation), and Jesus also died to free us from our sin (sanctification). Forgiveness is the first part of the equation. Sin separates us from God, but when we are saved, the relationship is restored. Freedom is the second part of the equation. When we are in a right relationship with God, then we begin to obey God from a heart of love. We're not only forgiven, we're free. We bear the fruits of the Spirit—love, joy, peace, patience, kindness, goodness, faithfulness, gentleness, and self-control.

What's so joyful about salvation and sanctification? Hebrews 12:1–2 fleshes this thought out more:

> Therefore, since we are surrounded by such a great cloud of witnesses, let us throw off everything that hinders and the sin that so easily entangles. And let us run with perseverance the race marked out for us, fixing our eyes on Jesus, the pioneer and perfecter of faith. For the joy set before him he endured the cross, scorning its shame, and sat down at the right hand of the throne of God.

"For the joy set before him [Jesus] endured the cross" (v. 2). That means joy is greater than shame. Shame is one of the most powerful emotions that exists. Nothing will debilitate and devastate and depress and embarrass more than shame. But the joy being talked about here is the joy of obeying the Father from a heart of love. The result of that obedience is that Jesus brings God's prodigal children home. The result of our living sanctified lives is that our joy is greater than any sorrow. As Christ works in our lives, we gradually become more and more like him. That's joy.

> *The result of our living sanctified lives is that our joy is greater than any sorrow.*

Think of it this way. Did Jesus say, "I have come to give you life, and life more average"?

Did Jesus say, "Abide in me, and you'll only bear a teensy little bit of fruit"?

Did Jesus say, "My divine power has granted to you just a few things pertaining to life and godliness"?

No. Of course not. Jesus promises us full and abundant life. Jesus offers us a bumper crop of fruit—fruit, more

211

fruit, and even much fruit. God makes big promises to us, and we can't be afraid of big answers. God uses big promises to describe our lives, and our joy is in being a son or daughter of the King of kings.

In 1 John 1:3–4, the apostle John says:

> We proclaim to you what we have seen and heard, so that you also may have fellowship with us. And our fellowship is with the Father and with his Son, Jesus Christ. We write this to make our joy complete.

There are two key concepts in that verse. The first is fellowship and the second is joy. John wrote to the early churches to reiterate for them that he and the other apostles actually saw and experienced Jesus firsthand. He wasn't a figment of their imagination. They saw him with their eyes; they touched his physical presence with their hands. They heard his voice. They ate the same fish and bread he did. Then Jesus was crucified and buried and rose from the dead—and the apostles saw Jesus again. That's what they're proclaiming.

And they're doing it for a specific reason—so that other believers may have fellowship with them, because their fellowship is with the Father and with his Son, Jesus Christ. It's like everybody is one big happy family—and we can be, because of Christ. Why are they proclaiming this? Two reasons: first, it's hard to have joy when family and friends are headed to hell instead of heaven; second, there's no greater joy than the lost being found.

See, for joy to be complete, we proclaim Jesus to others, and we do it so we all become part of God's family. We're adopted in as sons and daughters, we receive the joy of God and respond to God with this joy, and then we give away this joy to others. That's the fullness of joy. It doesn't come from receiving only. The greatest expressions of joy in our lives, the most meaningful moments, are when we take what's been given to us and then turn and give it to someone else.

That's our joy. We are greatly loved. We are restored to God the Father through the work of Jesus on the cross. Our joy is full because Jesus' joy is full. Our joy is full when we have fellowship with God and with one another. We live for their progress and joy in the faith. And the result of love working is joy, great joy, the fullness of joy.

> *The greatest expressions of joy in our lives, the most meaningful moments, are when we take what's been given to us and then turn and give it to someone else.*

This can take time, sure, and nobody likes to wait. But good things can come to those who wait.

If you'd like to watch Bull tell his family's story, go to ChrisConlee.net.

11

Nobody Likes to Wait

But love works over the long haul.

L ove worked big time in my friend Kelley Hendrix's life. But love took time to work, and that took a lot of patience on behalf of the people who loved and cared for and prayed for Kelley. I'll let Kelley tell you his story in his own words:

> When I look back on my life, I am amazed at the evidence of God's handprint. Even before I was born, he was setting things up so that I would become the man of God I am today. Jeremiah 1:5 says, "Before I formed you in the womb I knew you, before you were born I set you apart; I appointed you as a prophet to the nations."
>
> I was born in 1973 in Memphis, and my home life proved rocky at the start. My mother was a hurt and angry woman, and my father was an alcoholic. As a child, I witnessed many

horrible fights between my parents, and I was on the receiving end of some of my mother's anger due to my father's alcoholic ways. Their marriage just about broke apart. I was sexually abused once by a so-called family friend, which hurt me deeply. Fortunately, things grew better for a time, before they grew worse again.

After my parents separated, my dad got a visit from one of our pastors. Dad understood the only saving grace to be had was by surrendering his life to Christ, which he did. On that day, his desire to drink was taken away and he has never looked back. That radically changed my mother too. God restored my parents' marriage, and from that point onward my parents sought to be the most godly and loving parents they could possibly be.

My younger brother, Chris, is two years younger than me, and every time the doors to the church were open, Chris and I were there. Sunday. Wednesday. Vacation Bible school. Christian summer camp. We were even enrolled in a private school where God's Word was taught daily. My parents loved us and did their best to teach us how to live for God in hopes that we would not go down the same road they'd once traveled, which had caused them so much pain and misery in their own lives before they completely surrendered to Christ.

I'd been deeply wounded as a child, and the wounds had not yet healed as a teenager and young man. Unfortunately, a lot of the Christian influence that came my way was legalistic and rules-oriented. I developed a lot of head knowledge about God. I knew the steps of salvation. I prayed the sinner's prayer and was baptized. But my faith was limited. In my mind, God was someone who could give me things I wanted. I prayed so a girl would like me. I prayed to win a ballgame. I prayed to have a car. I prayed to have more money. My faith was about God giving me things so I could feel good right now.

When I was fifteen, I opened the door for alcohol to enter into my life, the one thing my folks had tried so hard to keep me from because it had wreaked such havoc in their own lives. I started to live a double life—acting one way at church and Christian school and another way when I went out and partied. Alcohol let me do whatever I wanted to do (everything my parents told me I couldn't or shouldn't do) and it allowed me to do it without the consequence of feeling guilty.

Over the next few years, Satan would use several of his "weapons of mass destruction" on me. At age eighteen, I began using steroids to pump up my vanity. At twenty-one, I was regularly smoking weed. At twenty-two, I was using crystal and cocaine. At twenty-four, ecstasy. All these weapons succeeded in slowly destroying my life, as well as ruining any relationships I cared about with family members and friends. Each drug slowly stripped me of all the things in life I had grown to love. My love for sports and athletics dissolved. My leadership abilities fell apart. Any relationship with God I'd once had grew muddied. I caused myself and a lot of other people a whole lot of pain and misery—and I even led my younger brother right along with me into the world of drugs.

Eventually, I flunked out of college. It was tough to get up and go to class after partying all night—go figure. I got a job working in our family business, a body shop, which had been started by my grandfather. I made a bit of cash and bought a new truck, a house, a boat, and a motorcycle. I began to build my own empire, but what I didn't know was I was setting myself up for failure. Everyone who truly cared about me saw what was happening and knew it was only a matter of time before it all came crashing down.

Through all this, my parents, family, and a few true friends continued to pray for me, that God would get my attention. He heard their prayers and he was on the move to do just that.

I was using heavily, and repeatedly, I wasn't able to make it into work, so my dad had no choice but to fire me. Chris and I started selling drugs, and we did this for some time. We made a lot of money and blew it all on drugs. It's a hard life, the path we had chosen. We ran in circles with people who were robbed and shot, we drove with drugs in our system, we got in trouble with the law, we watched friends die—you name it, we did it.

Chris and I got arrested in 2002 for possession. We had multiple drugs on us—meth, cocaine, weed, crystal—and we were looking at going to prison for a long time. The courts showed mercy to us, and the case was kicked out of court. But my life was still miserable. Not long after that, I went on a five-day cocaine binge. At the end of it, I was broke, hungry, exhausted, and sick. I went home to my parents' house and passed out. Within an hour, Dad woke me up. The family was gathered downstairs and held an intervention for me. I'd already tried rehab and it hadn't worked. But I agreed to go again. They packed me up at 3:30 in the morning and dropped me off at a recovery center. I sat in a room with the director and my dad.

My dad said, "Son, do you even know what day it is?"

I said yes.

Happy birthday, Dad!

It was my dad's fifty-first birthday.

I stayed at that recovery center for six months. God got ahold of my life at the center and became more real to me than he'd ever been before. Up to that point, my life had been about rules without relationship. I'd never fully surrendered my life to Christ or known him in a personal way. But in the center, I got to know God closely, intimately. My younger brother got his life together too—and he was ahead of me in his recovery. He was attending Highpoint Church by then, and was very involved in several men's Bible study groups. In a dream, God spoke to me, telling me to follow the example of my younger brother in the faith. So, I did that. I graduated from the program and came home a different man.

Frequently, people forget that recovery is never a solo event. Our families are on this journey with us. At a Sunday night service, my dad asked me to join him at the front of the meeting. I did. He told the story of the prodigal son—about how when the son finally came to his senses and came home, the father ran to him, embraced him, and gave him a ring for his finger. My dad brought out a ring and gave it to me as a sign his prodigal son had come home. That was in June 2004.

God gave me grace upon grace. He let me know he'd never ever left me, even when I strayed. And even though I'd messed so many things up, he still had great plans for my life. I went back to working for my dad and I followed my little brother around Highpoint Church, attending every men's Bible study we could. God was still doing a huge work of recovery in my life, helping me set down roots, and ultimately giving me a new passion and purpose in life to live for the Lord. Through the church singles' group, I met my wife, Jenny. We were married in April 2005, and we have five kids today.

During our second year of marriage, God put it on my heart to help some family members who were struggling with drug addiction. They saw something in me they wanted—to be sober and to have peace. So, I started a Bible study in our house. We started with two guys. Jenny cooked supper for everybody afterward. Two years later, we had twenty-five guys coming to our house—and Jenny was still cooking supper for everyone. That group eventually morphed into the Celebrate Recovery program we have at Highpoint today.

I'm still a leader in the ministry now, more than a decade after getting sober. God has used all the past hurts of my life—he's taken what was so horrible and dark and turned that around to where I use that platform to help others going through the same stuff. Over the years, we've witnessed countless stories of people coming to the Lord and having victory over their hurts, habits, and hang-ups.

My name is Kelley Hendrix, and I'm the prodigal son who came home and began to serve my Father in a surrendered and uncompromised way.

The Patience of Love

Celebrate Recovery has been one of the defining ministries of Highpoint Church. It's never been about "those" people; it's always about "us." Without Christ, all of us are addicted to sin in some way. We reached out to the city of Memphis with Celebrate Recovery, and we did a billboard campaign for a year that used Kelley's face. He was well-enough known in the underworld of Memphis that his picture alone would be a testimony. If Kelley could change, then anyone could change. All things are possible with Jesus Christ.

Love takes patience—have you noticed? God can bring about a big change in a person's life, but more times than not, people are slow to trust and respond to God's love through God's people. So, understanding the necessity of patience is a big need for us all because it's far too easy to grow impatient when it comes to loving people. God works on his time and he respects the time frame of each person involved. I find great comfort in Galatians 6:9, "Let us not become weary in doing good, for at the proper time we will reap a harvest if we do not give up."

It's a funny thing about being a prodigal . . . we have this misunderstanding that prodigals are the minority of us. But the reality is that it's incredibly easy for any of us to walk away from God (or to fail to connect with God in the first place). We're all just a few poor decisions away from rejecting what we know to be true.

The definition of a prodigal is simply someone who is running away from God instead of running toward God. And not every prodigal looks the same. Prodigals come in all different sizes, shapes, and lifestyles. Some people are overt prodigals, lost in their recklessness and rebellion. Others are rich prodigals, trapped in their cash and the pursuit of the success scene. Still others are clean-living prodigals, even churchgoing prodigals. They might be wise to the ways of the faith, yet mired in rule-following or bitterness. They're depending on their own goodness to save them, but it never will. Some prodigals appear put together and look down their noses at people who "look" lost—but they're running from God's grace just the same. Some people are lost in their badness while others are lost in their goodness. Either way, they're still lost.

When love works, we want to help move prodigals from where they are to where God wants them to be. We want to help prodigals find their way home to God—which is one of the main reasons for loving people in the first place. We extend God's love to them, and love shows them faith in action. Our love acts as God's calling card in their lives, letting them know they're not forgotten. God is always actively waiting for people to find their way home to him.

When Jesus told the parable of the prodigal son, it was actually the third in a string of parables he told. That's important to understand, because the three parables taken together show the overall context of what Jesus was saying. These three parables are found in Luke 15 and they give us a good picture of patience in loving others. So, let's look at them one at a time and see how patience factors into loving people. This is the mission of God.

The Lost Sheep

The first two verses of Luke 15 are often overlooked, but they're important because they set the stage for everything that comes next: "Now the tax collectors and sinners were all drawing near to hear him. And the Pharisees and the scribes grumbled, saying, 'This man receives sinners and eats with them'" (vv. 1–2 ESV).

Jesus was friends with all the wrong people for all the right reasons.

It's a context of complaining. The religious people of the day were finding fault with Jesus because he associated with sinful people. Jesus was friends with all the wrong people for all the right reasons. That's radical. Right there, those two verses can form the modern methodology of how to love people. Don't worry about what religious people think. Rather, be concerned with God's mission

222

of reaching people who are running away from him. The people who were *unlike* Jesus liked Jesus. But the religious people of the day didn't like Jesus liking the unliked.*

We need to camp on this point for a bit because in the religious community it's so easy to start seeing ourselves as better than other people. Hey—we don't do drugs. We don't sleep around. We don't lie and cheat and steal. We're nice folks—and it's nice that we're such nice folks. But when nice folks get around other nice folks, they have a horrible habit of not being nice. And that's the opposite of what Jesus would do!

What would Jesus do? He says things like . . .

"Hey, you're a glutton and a drunkard? I'll be your friend. I've been accused of being the very same things. But I'll help you find your way home to the Father."

"So, you're a prostitute? Nice people don't associate with you? Well, I'll be your friend. When you come into my presence, I won't tell you how bad you are. I'll see the best in you. I'll show you how you can be free and forgiven. I'll point you to a life that's full of joy and gladness and peace."

"So, you're a tax collector? A liar and a cheat? Come, let's have supper together. Let me show you a different way of living, a way that leads with kindness and compassion. Your old ways are behind you now. You and me together can change the world!"

That's what it looks like when love works. It works in such a phenomenal way that when people see such radical

*I'm thankful to Andy Stanley for his teachings on this subject.

love, they can't quite put two and two together. They know there's something different about you, but they can't quite explain it. They see hope in you. They see peace in you. Whatever you have, they want it.

Those two verses in Luke 15 show that sinners were coming to Jesus and were comfortable in his presence. Jesus spoke their language and introduced the gospel to them slowly in ways they could not only grasp with their minds but feel with their hearts. Then Jesus told the crowd the first parable. He said, "Suppose one of you has a hundred sheep and loses one of them. Doesn't he leave the ninety-nine in the open country and go after the lost sheep until he finds it? And when he finds it, he joyfully puts it on his shoulders and goes home. Then he calls his friends and neighbors together and says, 'Rejoice with me; I have found my lost sheep'" (Luke 15:4–6).

Everyone in the crowd could identify with that story. Theirs was an agrarian culture, and every sheep was important. If one sheep got lost, then of course you'd search high and low until you found it. The parable made perfect sense to Jesus' hearers.

The modern spiritual equivalent is searching for a person who goes from lost to found. When that happens, incredible joy results, as we talked about in the last chapter. That's why it's important to love people. That's why it's important to love and love and love and love—and keep on loving until a person is found. The ninety-nine righteous people don't need to be found. But the one lost sinner desperately needs finding. It might take a while for that lost person to be found—but oh, what joy there is when that happens.

May we always keep this perspective! Lost people are important. We need to stay in the midst of people who aren't religious, and we need to throw the doors of every Jesus-following church wide open, welcoming the disenfranchised, the marginalized, and sinners of every kind. Unfortunately, this is still extremely rare today. Too many churches conveniently prioritize discipleship over evangelism, but all true discipleship starts with evangelism. Yes, it's messy. Yes, it's out of our comfort zones. Yes, it requires patience and kindness—but yes, it is vitally important work!

The Lost Coin

Jesus' first parable about sheep and shepherds probably spoke more to the men in the crowd. But the next parable probably spoke more to the women. He said, "Or what woman, having ten silver coins, if she loses one coin, does not light a lamp and sweep the house and seek diligently until she finds it? And when she has found it, she calls together her friends and neighbors, saying, 'Rejoice with me, for I have found the coin that I had lost.' Just so, I tell you, there is joy before the angels of God over one sinner who repents" (Luke 15:8–10 ESV).

In that day, fathers would give their daughters ten coins as a wedding gift to be sewn into the folds of a headdress. These coins were valuable. If one got lost, then of course a woman would search until she found it. What would it be like today if the diamond fell out of your engagement ring? Would you just say, "Oh, whatever—I'll find it later," and walk out of the house?

No way. We've got to keep loving people, and keep loving people, and keep loving people—until they are found. That's where the joy emerges.

I mentioned that my older brother died in an accident in 1981 when he was eighteen years old. About a year and a half before he died, he developed a friendship with a guy named Billy Perry. Billy and my brother both golfed. They were on different teams, but they turned their rivalry into a friendship. Billy was just a teenager trying to live for Christ. He started influencing my brother, just being his friend, and through that process my brother came to know the Lord.

Billy is in his early fifties today. He lives in Memphis, and every now and then we'll bump into each other at a restaurant or coffee shop. What's the first thing that comes to my mind when I see Billy Perry? *Thank you!*

Thank you! Thank you! Thank you! Thank you for being on a mission to seek and save the lost. Thank you for loving people, and for not giving up on people, and for introducing people to Jesus!

From Billy's perspective, he looks back and doesn't think he did anything huge. He was just a teen trying to walk with the Lord and love God the best way he knew how. Billy didn't use any program to love my brother. He didn't memorize any script. He just lived for God. He received the love of God, he let this love flow through him, and he loved others with this love. I have the assurance of knowing my brother is in eternity with Christ because, more than thirty-five years ago, someone cared enough to love and lead my brother to Christ.

The Prodigal Son

Then Jesus told a third story. It's the longest, and is found in Luke 15:11–32. A good father had two sons. One day, the younger son went to his father and asked for his share of the inheritance early. In that day, a request like that was a slap in the face. It was as if the younger brother said to his father, "I wish you were already dead." Everyone who heard Jesus tell that story would have been offended. They'd have said, "Wow, can you imagine someone being so arrogant and rude?"

Every parent has done kind things for his or her kids, but there are times when our kids don't respond with kindness. A father will say, "I love you, son." But maybe that son is thirteen or fourteen and going through a rough patch, and says back with a sneer, "Yeah, well, I hate you, Dad." Such insolence or disrespect doesn't happen to that degree in every household. But it does happen, and I think most of us would respond the same way. If our kids came to us and told us to drop dead, we wouldn't give them money. We'd probably get into some sort of shouting match or impose some sort of discipline.

But the good father offered a kind response. He had his reasons—he wanted to build a bridge instead of burn one, so he gave his son what he asked for. If the father had cussed out the boy, that wouldn't have solved anything—and the son still would have left. The radical thing is that the way the father handled the son's leaving actually gave the boy an invitation to return. The relationship wasn't destroyed. Note how Romans 2:4 says, "The kindness of God leads you to repentance" (NASB). This is what the father showed to his son. The son didn't deserve kindness, but kindness can actually break through the hardness of a heart.

When people act immaturely toward us, oh, it fires us up and makes us so angry, and we want to return their immaturity with immaturity of our own. But then the situation just becomes ugly. This is a great life lesson: the madder you get, the dumber you get. The mature response is to respond to immaturity with kindness. Proverbs 15:1 says, "A gentle answer turns away wrath."

The son took his share of the inheritance and went to a different country, where he squandered all he had on reckless living. When he'd spent everything and his so-called friends had left, a severe famine arose in the country. The prodigal son grew hungry and got the only job he could find: feeding pigs. This job paid so little that the son longed to eat the pigs' food. This is important: the son began to be in need. We have to let people experience their need. If we keep enabling them to continue in their sin, then our actions actually delay their return. This is a hard reality, but most of us don't come to our senses until we realize how miserable we are, eating with the pigs. Hurts, habits, and hang-ups are normal for everyone, and if we think we're above that, then we're just lying to ourselves. It's where we all live. But we all have to come to a place of hitting rock bottom and coming to our senses. That's when we realize we can't do it on our own.

At last, the son came to his senses. He thought about home, how his father's servants all had food to spare. The boy decided to go home and apologize to his dad, saying he was no longer worthy to be called a son. He went home, but while he was a long way off, the father saw him, raced down the road to meet him, and embraced him. Then he threw a big party in honor of his son's homecoming.

It's such a beautiful picture when a prodigal at last says, "God, I can't do this anymore. I need you to forgive me and save me from my sin." There are actually two types of repentance. There's a worldly sorrow that leads to the first type of repentance—where we're only sorry that we got caught. If we hadn't been caught, then we wouldn't be sorry. Then there's a godly sorrow that leads to the second type of repentance—a true regret that leads to salvation and restoration. This is where we are truly sorry for our offenses and for the distance and separation and destruction that have been created. We agree with God, and God removes the distance, heals, cleanses, and restores us. The boy experienced the second kind of repentance.

Our responsibility in loving people is to wait for them. It's to always be looking down the road for their return. Practically speaking, we're called to pray for the prodigal while he's gone, to write notes and letters and send emails and texts that say, "Hey, I'm thinking of you. I love you. You're always welcome home." Our responsibility is that when they come to their senses, we're available. It's that simple. We don't say, "What were you thinking, you fool?" No, our responsibility is to say, "I'm so glad you came home."

When the older brother heard the news that his prodigal brother had come home, he wasn't happy. And when he found out that his father had thrown the boy a party, the older brother practically went through the roof. He sulked out in the fields by himself for a while, isolated in his bitterness. Then the good father went out to have a talk.

But he answered his father, "Look! All these years I've been slaving for you and never disobeyed your orders. Yet you never gave me even a young goat so I could celebrate with my friends. But when this son of yours who has squandered your property with prostitutes comes home, you kill the fattened calf for him!"

"My son," the father said, "you are always with me, and everything I have is yours. But we had to celebrate and be glad, because this brother of yours was dead and is alive again; he was lost and is found." (Luke 15:29–32)

Imagine that moment. The prodigal's return was *heartwarming*. But the older brother's response was *heartbreaking*. The prodigal's return is a picture of repentance—he had a change of heart that led to a change of direction. But the older brother's response is a picture of hypocrisy.

The father encouraged the older son not to be right, but to be right relationally.

Fortunately, the father's response to both of his sons is a picture of divine grace. God gives us what we do not deserve: kindness.

The father didn't chastise either son for what they did wrong. Instead, he called each son toward a better way of living. He praised the prodigal son for returning to his senses. And he encouraged the older son to remain closely in the relationship that was already established. The father encouraged the older son not to be right, but to be right *relationally*.

That's our calling too—to be used by Jesus Christ to help bring all the prodigal children home to the Father. That's our purpose, privilege, and pleasure in life.

Always Searching for Their Return

My prayer is for us to always be patient with people. Let us always persevere with people when they are in a prodigal season, always longing for them to come home to Jesus. Let us always be searching for their return, like we're looking for lost sheep or lost coins. We are willing and ready to run down the road toward them with our arms open wide, saying, "Welcome home! I'm so glad you returned!"

As we've seen throughout this book, we receive the love of Jesus, then return his love back to God, then love other people with God's love. How about you? What will you do today to prove love works? Your plan doesn't need to be difficult, but it might have tremendously positive lasting implications for you, your family, and even a lot of people.

If you'd like to watch Kelley tell his
story, go to ChrisConlee.net.

12

When Love Heals

Love will work in your life today.

In the late 1990s, a Memphis physician named Dr. Dan Griffin was praying that a new sort of church would come to his city: a church that loved people wholeheartedly in the name of Jesus; a church that continually focused on "outsiders" more than "insiders"; a church that communicated the thoughts and heart of Jesus to people who had no idea what Jesus is all about.

Dan was in his mid-fifties then, and going to a traditional church at the time, but in his words, the church was "filled with old ladies with blue hair who didn't care about skateboarders with green hair." It was no simple twist on words. He and his wife, Fay, held a Disciple Now program at their house, where unsaved kids came to their home to be introduced to matters of the faith. Dan and Fay asked the leader to send them "the meanest group of boys they had." One of the kids had green hair and was a skateboarder. He sat at the Griffins' piano and played classical music, of all things, and the Griffins loved that kid with all the love they had. But the sad thing is they weren't sure if this boy would have been welcomed at their church.

Several times in the past, the Griffins had invited unsaved people to their church, hoping they would encounter Jesus. People came, mostly to be polite, but they never came back. One woman sat through the service, then said, "You know, the people were kind to me, but I had no idea what they were talking about."

So, Dr. Dan and his wife kept praying. A few months later, they were at a banquet for an organization called Life Choices that supports unwed mothers. It was at this banquet that God put it in Dan's heart to start a church. He made a decision to set up a meeting with the pastor at his church and explore the possibilities. His pastor knew a young pastor up in Ohio who felt a burden to start a new kind of church. Dan took the initiative to call that pastor and share his burden.

Strangely enough, the young pastor was highly intrigued by what Dr. Dan had to say—I know this, because that young pastor was me.

Here's what had been happening from my end of things. Karin and I had been involved in a church in Ohio for a couple of years by then. It was a tremendous training ground for us, but we sensed that the Lord was calling us to begin a new work somewhere.

Just before Dr. Dan called me, I'd gone to the Catalyst conference held at North Point Community Church in

Atlanta. It's a conference designed for pastors under age forty and focused on reaching the next generation. At this conference, God gave me his vision and calling to start Highpoint Church. I didn't have the specifics at that point, just a word from God to do it. All during that conference, I was burdened for Memphis. I'd had this burden for a while, even though we weren't living in Memphis. Karin and I had grown up there, and it still felt like home. But we were open to whatever location and call God led us to.

During that conference, I prayed that if God wanted me to go to Memphis, then the call would need to come from the Lord. I wouldn't seek a church in Memphis on my own initiative. Instead, I prayed the specific, unlikely prayer that someone from Memphis would call me and ask me to come start a church in that city. About five months later, I wrote in my journal one morning, asking God to either release me from the burden to go to Memphis or to please recommunicate to me in this powerful, specific way that Memphis was precisely where God wanted us to go.

Exactly fifteen minutes after I wrote those things in my journal, Dr. Dan Griffin phoned me. He told me he'd been praying for more than five years about the need for a church in Memphis that would reach the next generation and people of diversity. I was blown away because Dr. Dan and I had never met. I read to him from my journal what I'd just written, then said, "Well, I don't claim to be the smartest man in the world, but I still believe 2 plus 2 equals 4."

Those initial conversations and meetings with Dan led to the start of Highpoint Church about a year later. And the Griffins' own story is an integral piece of the church's beginning because they became our first members. The

Griffins were established at their own church. They loved Southern Gospel music, and their church had an organ and a choir and all the things they loved. But they were willing to give up their own preferences for the sake of loving people who had other preferences. Listen: The message of the gospel is always timeless. It never changes. But methodology needs to change with the times. If an organ and a choir weren't going to reach people, then the Griffins wanted the methodology that was going to work.

Love works.

That was the simple idea we founded this new church on. And the Lord has done some extraordinary things throughout the years. The Griffins sowed selfless seeds of faith, and because of that, they've helped usher in an enormous spiritual harvest. They became tireless workers in our new church. They gave of their own finances and time. Fay worked in the nursery all the time. Later, she was one of the primary movers and shakers who led the outreach to Overton High School. Dan did everything else that could be done. He taught classes, mentored people, prayed, and served as a trustee. That same woman who'd once visited the Griffins' other church ended up coming to Highpoint, where she was saved.

Why does the Griffins' story matter? I say this with the utmost respect, but you'd never look at the Griffins and think, *That's the couple God's going to use to start the most relevant and relentless church in Memphis.* They were faithful people in their fifties who personally loved their traditions, but they sacrificed the preferences of insiders for the preferences of outsiders. The Griffins don't exactly look like early adopters, but they've reached more imperfect people than anyone I know. One day in heaven, they'll meet countless people of diversity, people with crazy hair colors and tattoos and piercings who thank them for creating a safe place to hear a dangerous message.

The love that the Griffins had for the city of Memphis mattered. And, in conclusion, that's the emphasis I want to focus on. We've talked about a lot of things in this book, but if I could close with one thought, it would be this: *Your love for people matters today.* Receiving God's love matters. Responding to God's love matters. Giving God's love matters. Love matters because love works.

Five Ways We Prove Love Works

In these closing pages, the specific question in front of you is this: Who will you love, and how will you best love them? In order to prove love works, what will love require of you?

Only you can answer that question. You answer it in prayer, and you answer it by looking at your circle of influence. God's command isn't for you to know more; it's to love more.

Why make it more complicated than this? When we choose to love God and love others, the bulk of our problems are solved. The biggest

> *God's command isn't for you to know more; it's to love more.*

problem in the world is that the thing we want to work the most is working the least—love! But God has an answer for that, and it's not a new answer. It's an answer best expressed through friends applying these five relational principles.

1. As friends, we encourage each other.

The book of Hebrews encourages us to turn toward the living God. In doing so, we're to encourage our friends not to turn away from God. "But encourage one another daily, as long as it is called 'Today,' so that none of you may be hardened by sin's deceitfulness" (Heb. 3:13).

What does it look like to encourage a friend? It means we put into them what's missing. When one is discouraged, then courage has been removed. So, it's our job to strengthen them with courage. We continually inspire our friends to walk a step closer to Christ. We remind them that God never forgets us nor forsakes us. We inspire our friends with confidence by lifting them up and not bringing them down.

Encouragement is often spelled two different ways: *time* and *talk*. It takes both to build an encouraging friendship.

2. As friends, we spur each other on toward love and good deeds.

Hebrews 10:24–25 says, "And let us consider how we may spur one another on toward love and good deeds, not giving up meeting together, as some are in the habit of doing, but encouraging one another—and all the more as you see the Day approaching."

This is a picture of friends who know you well enough to intervene when you aren't doing well. Faithful friends are willing to risk offending for the sake of replacing bad habits with good habits. This is a clear delineation between being an acquaintance and a friend.

Connection happens by choice, not convenience. That's one of the many reasons we need to spur, stimulate, and even irritate one another to love and good deeds. The primary reason we must be intentional and proactive is because friendships influence a person's faithfulness or faithlessness. Friendships can make or break us. We were never meant to do this life or faith alone. It's impossible to fulfill the Greatest Commandment and the New Commandment of loving one another without friends being the primary recipients of our love.

None of us long for casual and convenient friendships. All of us long for loving and loyal friendships. The longing of our soul is to be fully known yet still fully loved. We want people to be with us through the good, bad, and ugly. We need to borrow the faith of our friends when we're going through adversity. We need friends who keep believing when we want to quit or give up. We need friends who coach us when we need to be coached. We need friends who are strong when we are weak. And if that is what we need, then we need to be that for others.

3. As friends, we restore one another in a spirit of gentleness.

Galatians 6:1 says, "Brothers and sisters, if someone is caught in a sin, you who live by the Spirit should restore that person gently. But watch yourselves, or you also may be tempted."

Jesus brings up our pasts only to heal them. Our failures are not final; our failures are forgiven. And our response to our failures helps determine our futures. Will we continually make the same mistakes? Will we continually return to our familiar sins? Or will we allow Christ to remake us in his image?

If a friend sins, we aren't to condemn that friend. Instead, modeling Christ, we are to gently point that person toward the truth. We're not to approach our friend with superiority or self-righteousness. Instead, we're to walk circumspectly, knowing that the same sin can tempt us in a similar way.

Our friends will let us down, sure. But resentment doesn't work. Show me someone who's both resentful and healthy, and I'll show you an igloo in Hawaii. We are called to continually forgive people. We release them from any offenses toward us. Replace the pain with God's peace.

4. As friends, we bear one another's burdens.

Galatians 6:2 says, "Carry each other's burdens, and in this way you will fulfill the law of Christ."

What does it look like to carry your friend's burdens? It involves creating a culture of trust, empathy, leadership, and loyalty. We're providing a safe place for them to be able to talk about what's really happening. We're saying, "How's your walk with God going? How's your soul? How are your relationships doing—the ones that mean the most to you?"

How do most people encounter Christ? They encounter Christ through us. We are the ones who bear the burdens. We are the ones who walk with people through the tragedy, through the loss, through the grieving. God uses our presence to be the manifestation of his peace. More times than not, it's not about the words we say but about the tears we cry and the hugs we give.

When I walk through seasons of crisis with people as their pastor, people seldom remember what I say to them.

But years later, they remember that I was there. Nothing communicates more than our presence during the highs and lows of life. There are moments in life when we know and they know we can't fix it, but it's in these moments that our presence and prayers matter most.

And friends also are aware of what they *can't* do. This might sound counterintuitive, but friends aren't called to fix other friends. Rather, we're called to point people toward Jesus—he's the One who heals and restores.

5. As friends, we live for one another's progress and joy in the faith.

Philippians 1:25 says, "Convinced of this, I know that I will remain, and I will continue with all of you for your progress and joy in the faith."

This means that friends persevere with one another. When the going gets tough, friends are patient with each other. We don't walk out the side door when hard times arise. We believe the best about our friends at all times. Our belief goes beyond their performance. We understand the challenges of life, but we're committed to helping our friends over the wall. These are the types of friends who have a "No Man Left Behind" mantra.

We know our friends' weaknesses, but we love them for their strengths. Our greatest need is for a band of brothers (or sisters) to fight the good fight together and to run the race together. The battle and the race are impossible as a solo act. Different friends run different legs of the race with us. I'm forever indebted and grateful for the friends who will finish the race with me.

Ultimately, Jesus changed the world forever with twelve friends who lived for one another's progress and joy in the faith.

The Rest of My Story

I've told you bits and pieces of my story throughout this book, and how so much of my story revolves around healing from broken love. Well, there's more to this story—and I tell it as a means of encouragement for you in this book's final pages. Broken love doesn't need to remain broken.

A few years back, when my son was twelve and my daughter was ten, I started closely examining my own life, wondering if I was destined to repeat the failures of broken love. Specifically, I wanted to guard against becoming like my dad when he'd been at his worst, particularly when it came to me being hyper-driven as a parent. So, I took my kids and my wife, Karin, on an unusual family vacation. We went to see a counselor outside of San Antonio. I know—fun, right? It definitely wasn't Disney's happiest place on earth, nor was it anyone's preferred vacation. But it was an invaluable investment in the future. My kids didn't fully appreciate it then, but today they'd say it was a game-changer.

In one counseling session, we were doing some role-playing. My son, Mark, is a classic strong-willed child, and sometimes he butts heads with Karin. So, in the session, Mark and Karin were replaying an argument they'd had, except this time they were both imagining themselves in the shoes of the other person, saying what the other person would say.

They played out the scene, and afterward the counselor debriefed each person. My son went first. The counselor asked Mark what he felt when he imagined himself in his mother's shoes. Mark answered, seeing his mother through eyes of love, and then he teared up. My wife broke down too. They hugged and embraced, and it was clear each person had grown through the session.

At the end of our time, the counselor asked us for any concluding thoughts on how the counseling had helped. Mark didn't say anything at first, but he acted like he was taking off a backpack and tossing it across the room. We asked him what that was about, and he said, "Well, I'm finally getting that monkey off my back." That's when I broke down.

I mean, I just *wept*.

The burden of broken love was gone. Mark's burden. My burden. My family's burden. We weren't destined to repeat the same mistakes of gen-

> *All throughout this world, love is broken. But it doesn't need to stay that way. We can all know and say and live out this amazing truth: love works.*

erations past. Our family was winning. We were proving love works! Love had been redefined for us, and we could do this; we could love one another. We could live in a better story.

The same invitation is our incredible calling as believers of Jesus. When we follow the way of love, we reap the excellent rewards, and others around us do too. All throughout this world, love is broken. But it doesn't need to stay that way. We can *all* know and say and live out this amazing truth: love works.

There's more to the story with my parents too.

My parents were initially married for thirty-four very difficult years, and during those years, my father was unfaithful and unpredictably angry. I doubt if they were happily married to begin with, and the tragedy of losing my brother pushed them further apart. They coped in their own ways, grieving differently and compartmentalizing their feelings. Eventually, they got divorced.

After about three years of being divorced, they decided to get remarried. They missed each other. Or at least, they missed the idea of one another. They asked me to officiate their wedding, and I did. God had gripped my life tightly by then. I was walking with the Lord, heading toward pastoral ministry and just finishing up seminary.

This second time, their marriage lasted less than two years. Dad was unfaithful to my mom again, so they got divorced again. My dad decided to marry the woman he was being unfaithful with. I went over to their house a few days before the ceremony, and he and I had a hard conversation. I said, "Dad, I think you're making the wrong choice. This choice is going to have a ripple effect. It's going to take you further and further away from your family and just create more boundaries." I was married to Karin by then, and Mark had been born and Annika was soon to come. Dad's new fiancée didn't seem to like us all very much. I think she felt threatened because our presence was a constant reminder to her of my dad's other life.

Dad said, "I understand, and I'm sorry. But this is what I'm going to do. You do what you need to do, and I'll do what I need to do."

That felt like a throat punch to me. I walked out of his house thinking, *Wow, he just chose this other woman—one*

*in a line of many—over his family, his children, and his grand-
children.* Karin and I talked extensively when I got home,
and we asked ourselves how we could have a relationship
with my dad anymore. But we made the decision, regardless
of what he'd done wrong, that we were not going to reject
him. If we didn't love him, then who would? If we pulled
away, then who was going to reach him for Christ? We
didn't want any greater strain in the relationship than there
already was. Karin and I decided we would redefine the
relationship as best we could and just love him anyway. We
would give him appropriate access to our children and let
him enjoy the privileges and benefits of being a granddad.

My mother didn't fare too well financially in the second
divorce. So, Karin and I decided to care for her. We built
a little guest house beside our house, and my mom lived
in that.

Dad got married. He'd come over occasionally to our
house—usually just him, but not his new wife—and he'd
watch a ballgame or have a meal with us. Karin and I always
tried to create an environment where he felt accepted and
not rejected. Dad thought the world of his grandson, and
when Annika came along, he was over the moon about
her. Dad and his wife stayed married for eight years, then
got divorced.

Then my mom and dad decided to get remarried again.
My father hadn't changed much, but my mom was following Jesus and wanted to love others in whatever ways Jesus
pointed her to. It wasn't a new faith for my mom, but it was
a renewed faith. I asked her what she thought of getting
married to my dad for a third time. She said, "Honestly,
I'm over him. But something good can still come of this. If

I marry him again, then that might be the only chance he has to meet Jesus. I think this might be the best chance of our family ever being healed and reunited. If I love him, then he can experience more of what God is doing for him, and I believe that's what God wants me to do."

So, I officiated again. I'm the only person I know to officiate his own parents' wedding twice! At the ceremony, my dad had no problem making fun of himself. He gave a little speech where he talked about how he was an imperfect man, and the relationship he had with my mom was "messed up." But "at least we're trying again," he said.

I took the microphone, took off my pastor's hat, and spoke directly to my dad, saying, "Dad, my mother is the toughest woman I've ever known, largely because you're the biggest pain in the rear I've ever known. But here she is, willing to love you again. Dad, if you ever divorce her again, I will literally kick your you-know-what."

My parents stayed married this third time.

My dad started coming to church with my mom, little by little in the beginning, but then more regularly. At first, my dad was just showing up and seemed to be the same guy he'd always been. Then things began to change for him.

I did a sermon series called "Overcoming That Voice" where I invited people to look at influential persons in their lives, specifically people who'd influenced them negatively. Before I started the series, I went to my dad and asked him if I could use some stories from my growing-up years as illustrations. I was going to teach the series from a place of healing, not hurting, and I'd tell the stories respectfully. He said yes, he trusted me, so I started teaching the series. At the end of every message, I invited people to trust Jesus.

One day in the middle of this series, my son, Mark, went over to my dad's house. My dad said, "Hey, Mark, when your dad leads people in that prayer for salvation at the end of each service, how do you know the prayer works?"

Mark asked, "Did you pray that prayer, Bready?" (Mark called him by his nickname, just like everybody else did.)

And my dad said, "Well, why do you think I asked the question?"

At age seventy-one, my father chose to follow Jesus. Love began to work in his life. He'd lived for so many years with love not working. But now it began to work. I asked my dad about the change in him, just to hear about it directly from him, and he said, "Listen, if anybody needs to be forgiven, it's me. I don't want to live the life I've always lived." I asked my mom about it, and she said, "Chris, this is legit this time."

At my father's request, my son Mark baptized my father. There wasn't a dry eye in the church. In my father's seventies, he saw love work in his life and he came full circle. It took a wife to keep loving him and marry him three times, his children to keep the relational bridges built, his grandchildren to love him and pray for him and be loved by him, and his church to pray for him, accept him, and love him. But in the end—love worked!

Eighteen months after he'd accepted the Lord, when my dad was seventy-three, he went out one afternoon and played a round of golf. He shot a 69 and felt great. Thanks to my dad's independent upbringing, he'd always had a tender spot for young people. He was always encouraging the next generation, wanting them to succeed. A high schooler who worked in the clubhouse had just graduated and was heading off to college, so Dad went out and bought her a cake and a congratulations card on behalf of all the regulars at the club to help celebrate her journey forward. He said a few words in the clubhouse, gave her the cake, then immediately fell over from a massive heart attack.

The paramedics worked on him, and he went to the hospital in an ambulance. I reached him at the hospital. He was still in the ambulance, and the paramedics were still working on him. I held my father's hand and in that instant I knew that he was already gone. I whispered under my breath, "I've lost him."

But just at that moment, as clearly as I've ever heard God speak, the voice of the Holy Spirit said to me, *I've got him.*

That was my peace. God held my father close. Love had worked. Love had healed.

It was a tragic and unexpected death, but he died doing what he loved most: playing golf and showing others kindness. His last act on earth had been to throw a celebration for another person. It was an act of genuine kindness. It had taken my dad a lifetime, but he finally lived a life that proved love works.

I tell you these last two stories just to show you that I've seen love work in my own life. It wasn't head knowledge that brought my dad to the Lord. Oh, sure, there was some truth he needed to know. But it was his experiences with God's people who showed him unconditional love that made all the difference. My dad went from broken to healed. He went from shame to forgiveness. He went from guilt to peace. The only way all those years of brokenness could be healed was by love.

And that's the message I want to leave with you.

The relationships that are strained in your life today can be redefined. Don't give up on people. Don't stop loving them. Keep reaching out. Keep praying for people. Keep showing them the unconditional love of Christ.

Who do you need to love today? Go to them in friendship. Go to them and encourage them. Go to them to spur them on toward love and good deeds. Go to them and restore each other in a spirit of gentleness. Go to them and bear one another's burdens. Go to them and live for each other's progress and joy in the faith. And remember, always—

Love works.

If you'd like to watch Dr. Dan tell his story, go to ChrisConlee.net.

If God has used this book in a significant way in your life, please go to ChrisConlee.net and tell us your story.

Acknowledgments

I've always seen myself to be a person with a limited skill set, so please believe me when I say that this book wouldn't exist without an incredible team. It's my hope and prayer that each member of this team receives the fulfillment and joy of hearing the Lord speak these words over them: "Well done, good and faithful servant."

My wife, Karin, for being my best friend and soulmate. You inspire me daily to pursue God in order to lead you and love you in a way that's worthy of being your husband. You have the highest character and are the most competent person I've ever known.

My son, Mark, for the privilege of being your dad and your buddy. You may be named after me, but you're an original in every respect. Thank you for using your charisma and sense of humor to make our family less serious and more fun. I can't wait to see how God uses your winsome ways and words to prove love works.

My daughter, Annika, for the privilege of being your dad and your conversationalist. You are truly brilliant with a touch of blonde. You keep me thinking deeply and smiling constantly. I love how you live with a sense of divine purpose. You've been hardwired by God to be a storyteller. I can't wait to see how God uses your spoken and written words to prove love works.

My team:

Andy Savage, for being the cofounder of Highpoint Church and one of my best friends. Thank you for maximizing my strengths and minimizing my weaknesses. You are truly gifted and great in many areas, but I want to highlight your top three. You are an incredible husband, an influential dad, and an inspiring communicator. You heard it here first, everyone . . . Andy Savage will be one of the leading voices and authors on marriage and parenting in the near future.

Sue Strydom, for redefining the role and value of an executive assistant. Thank you for representing me with class and professionalism. Thank you for believing in my dreams and helping bring them into reality. The Conlees can't thank you enough for all the ways you serve us and bless us. You are an invaluable teammate and friend.

The Highpoint team, for being the vision carriers who maximize and multiply the vision of *Love Works* every single day. You are relentless in your pursuit of godliness, giftedness, and greatness. Thank you for leading the city of Memphis to rediscover faith, hope, and love.

Movements are never the result of a great individual; they're always the result of a great team.

The Highpoint family because, ultimately, this book exists because *Love Works* is your vision and story. You are changing Memphis one life at a time by proving only love covers a multitude of sins, only love never fails, and only love works. It's my prayer this is just the beginning locally, nationally, and globally. Thank you for the privilege of being your pastor.

Greg Johnson and Marcus Brotherton, thank you for believing in me and using your experience and expertise to make this dream come true. Greg, thank you for representing me and putting this team together. Marcus, thank you for your humble and prayerful approach to this book. You truly have a gift with words and have enhanced this book in countless ways.

Jeff Rosenblum, I have many friends, but few I respect, appreciate, and love as much as you. I pray for this book to bless people around this world, but I pray it starts with you.

About the Author

Chris Conlee is the lead pastor of Highpoint Church in Memphis, Tennessee, where he is inspired to lead a movement of people committed to loving God, loving people, and making disciples—because only love works.

He holds a bachelor's degree in communication from the University of Memphis and a master's of divinity from Mid-America Baptist Theological Seminary.

His highly acclaimed book, *Priority Time: Addicted to God's Word*, has revolutionized people's understanding of how to have a "quiet time" and is a valuable resource for anyone who desires to spend time with God daily through the Word and in prayer.

Chris and his wife, Karin, have two teenagers, Mark and Annika, who do everything they can to keep life interesting.

www.chrisconlee.net
www.highpointmemphis.com

HIGHP◉INT
C H U R C H

A PEOPLE WHO PROVE LOVE WORKS.

Follow the movement:

- Watch our pastors' messages at highpointmemphis.com/loveworks

- Go to chrisconlee.net/loveworks now to receive Chris's *30 Day Priority Time Devotionals* for **FREE**

- Watch our Going Public stories of life change at highpointmemphis.com/media

- Listen to our music at highpointworship.com/loveworks

Highpoint East Memphis	Highpoint Collierville	Highpoint Arlington
Sundays at 9:15am & 11am	Sundays at 9:15am & 11am	Sundays at 10am & 11:30am
6000 Briarcrest Ave	1035 E Winchester Blvd	11015 Highway 64
Memphis, TN 38120	Collierville, TN 38017	Arlington, TN 38002

HIGHPOINTMEMPHIS.COM

Resources from Chris & Karin Conlee

chrisconlee.net
ⓕ /conleechris
ⓘ @conleechris
ⓧ @chrisconlee

karinconlee.com
ⓕ /karin.conlee
ⓘ @karinlconlee
ⓧ @karinconlee

Go to **chrisconlee.net/loveworks** now to receive Chris's *30 Day Priority Time Devotionals* for **FREE.**

....

Subscribe to these podcasts hosted by Chris & Karin at **chrisconlee.net**

....

Discover your purpose without the pressure.
Go to **karinconlee.com** now to order Karin's book, *Miss Perfect.*

....

Invite Chris or Karin to speak at your next event.
Chris and Karin—individually or together—are available to speak to your church, nonprofit, or business.
• For Chris, go to chrisconlee.net/speaking
• For Karin, go to karinconlee.com/booking